**SHORT WA...**
**MADE EAS...**

# SUFFOLK AND ESSEX COAST AND HEATHS

Ordnance Survey

# Contents

| | | |
|---|---|---|
| Getting outside on the Suffolk and Essex coast and heaths | | 6 |
| We smile more when we're outside | | 8 |
| Respecting the countryside | | 10 |
| Using this guide | | 11 |
| **Walk 1** | Oulton Broad | **14** |
| **Walk 2** | Southwold | **20** |
| Photos | Scenes from the walks | 26 |
| **Walk 3** | Dunwich | **28** |
| **Walk 4** | Aldeburgh and the River Alde | **34** |
| Photos | Wildlife interest | 40 |
| **Walk 5** | Orford and the River Ore | **42** |
| **Walk 6** | Sutton Hoo | **48** |
| **Walk 7** | Dedham and Flatford | **54** |
| Photos | Cafés and pubs | 60 |
| **Walk 8** | Colchester to Wivenhoe | **62** |
| **Walk 9** | West Mersea | **68** |
| **Walk 10** | Maldon | **74** |
| Credits | | 80 |

| | |
|---|---|
| Map symbols | Front cover flap |
| Accessibility and what to take | Back cover flap |
| Walk locations | Inside front cover |
| Your next adventure? | Inside back cover |

2  Short Walks Made Easy

---

## Walk 1

### OULTON BROAD

**Distance**
2 miles / 3.2 km

**Time**
1¼ hours

GO BY TRAIN CATCH A BUS

**Start/Finish**
Carlton Marshes Nature Reserve

**Parking**  NR33 8HU
Carlton Marshes Visitor Centre car park

**Cafés/pubs**
At the visitor centre; Ivy House Country Hotel

**The southern-most of the Broads; a wonderful wetland nature reserve**

Page 14

# Walk 2

## SOUTHWOLD

**Distance**
3.1 miles/5km

**Time**
1¾ hours  *CATCH A BUS*

**Start/Finish**
Southwold Pier

**Parking** IP18 6BN
Southwold Pier car park

**Cafés/pubs**
Southwold

**Pier, promenade, sandy beach; marsh grazing; town and lighthouse**

Page 20

# Walk 3

## DUNWICH

**Distance**
3.4 miles/5.4km

**Time**
2 hours

**Start/Finish**
Dunwich

**Parking** IP17 3EN
Dunwich Beach car park

**Cafés/pubs**
Flora Tea Rooms; The Ship

**A city that fell into the sea; monastery ruins; Leper Chapel; great pub**

Page 28

# Walk 4

## ALDEBURGH AND THE RIVER ALDE

**Distance**
4 miles/6.5km

**Time**
2¼ hours  *CATCH A BUS*

**Start/Finish**
Aldeburgh

**Parking** IP15 5DE
Fort Green car park

**Cafés/pubs**
Aldeburgh

**Peaceful River Alde and Aldeburgh Beach; Moot Hall and Town Steps**

Page 34

Contents  3

## Walk 5

### ORFORD AND THE RIVER ORE

**Distance**
3.5 miles/5.7km

**Time**
2 hours

**Start/Finish**
Orford

**Parking** IP12 2NU
Quay Street car park

**Cafés/pubs**
Orford

**Charming village; castle; popular bakery; Cold War relic; lovely river**

Page 42

## Walk 6

### SUTTON HOO

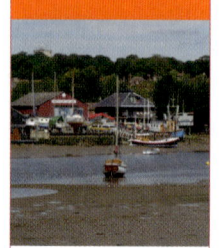

**Distance**
2.9 miles/4.6km

**Time**
1¾ hours  *CATCH A BUS*

**Start/Finish**
Sutton Hoo

**Parking** IP12 3DJ
National Trust Sutton Hoo car park

**Cafés/pubs**
National Trust café

**Britain's finest Anglo-Saxon treasure find; parkland; Deben views**

Page 48

## Walk 7

### DEDHAM AND FLATFORD

**Distance**
4 miles/6.4km

**Time**
2¼ hours  *CATCH A BUS*

**Start/Finish**
Dedham

**Parking** CO7 6DH
Mill Lane car park

**Cafés/pubs**
Dedham; National Trust café, Flatford

**Constable country walk in the Stour Valley along the Suffolk-Essex border**

Page 54

4   Short Walks Made Easy

## Walk 8

### COLCHESTER TO WIVENHOE

**Distance**
4.2 miles/6.7km

**Time**
2½ hours

*GO BY TRAIN CATCH A BUS*

**Start** Colchester Town Station
**Finish** Wivenhoe Station

**Parking** CO2 7EF
Britannia Car Park

**Cafés/pubs**
Colchester; Wivenhoe

Station-to-station walk; Roman capital; River Colne; Wivenhoe Trail

Page 62

## Walk 9

### WEST MERSEA

**Distance**
4.9 miles/7.9km

**Time**
2¾ hours

*CATCH A BUS*

**Start/Finish**
West Mersea

**Parking** CO5 8DA
Seaview car park

**Cafés/pubs**
West Mersea

Beach huts, coast road, and field paths; Britain's most easterly inhabited isle

Page 68

## Walk 10

### MALDON

**Distance**
4 miles/6.4km

**Time**
2¼ hours

*CATCH A BUS*

**Start/Finish**
Maldon

**Parking** CM9 5QP
White Horse Lane car park

**Cafés/pubs**
Maldon

Byrhtnoth and the Vikings; Promenade Park; the Maldon Mud Race

Page 74

Contents  5

# GETTING OUTSIDE ON THE SUFFOLK AND ESSEX COAST AND HEATHS

❝❞
Expansive skies and far-reaching seascapes lie in wait at Southwold, Dunwich and West Mersea

OS Champion
Natasha Sones

Dunwich Beach

A very warm welcome to the new Short Walks Made Easy guide to the Suffolk and Essex Coast and Heaths — what a fantastic selection of leisurely walks we have for you!

Sandy and shingle beaches, lonely marshland, myriad tidal creeks and charming seaside villages are just a few of the fascinating characteristics of the Suffolk and Essex Coast and Heaths National Landscape — an area of outstanding natural beauty that stretches from Oulton Broad, near Lowestoft, to Maldon, in Essex. Expansive skies and far-reaching seascapes lie in wait at Southwold, Dunwich and West Mersea. Intricate inlets and tidal islets form the backdrop to the walks at Orford, where there are relics of a Cold War listening station, and Maldon, site of a fearsome Viking battle. Salt marsh and peaceful, lazily meandering riversides can be followed at Aldeburgh and Orford.

Near Lowestoft, Oulton Broad is the southernmost of the Norfolk and Suffolk Broads, the walk here treading the Angles Way around the wetland nature reserve of Carlton Marshes. At Dunwich, discover the story of the city that was claimed by the sea and venture across the heathland common behind the beach. You can stroll in the parkland at Sutton Hoo, site of Britain's richest Anglo-Saxon burial, to fine views over the River Deben; while in Dedham Vale, the walk visits several of the Stour Valley sites captured by John Constable in his most famous paintings. From historic Colchester, there's a fine station-to-station walk along the River Colne to Wivenhoe.

**Natasha Sones,**
**OS Champion**

## WE SMILE MORE
## WHEN WE'RE OUTSIDE

Maldon

8  Short Walks Made Easy

# Whether it's a short walk during our lunch break or a full day's outdoor adventure, we know that a good dose of fresh air is just the tonic we all need.

At Ordnance Survey (OS), we're passionate about helping more people to get outside more often. It sits at the heart of everything we do, and through our products and services, we aim to help you lead an active outdoor lifestyle, so that you can live longer, stay younger and enjoy life more.

We firmly believe the outdoors is for everyone, and we want to help you find the very best Great Britain has to offer. We are blessed with countryside that is beautiful and unique, with a rich and varied landscape. There are coastal paths to meander along, woodlands to explore, open country to roam, and cities to uncover. Our trusted source of inspirational content is bursting with ideas for places to go, things to do and easy beginner's guides on how to get started.

It can be daunting when you're new to something, so we want to bring you the know-how from the people who live and breathe the outdoors. To help guide us, our team of awe-inspiring OS Champions share their favourite places to visit, hints and tips for outdoor adventures, as well as tried and tested accessible, family- and wheelchair-friendly routes. We hope that you will feel inspired to spend more time outside and reap the physical and mental health benefits that the outdoors has to offer. With our handy guides, paper and digital mapping, and exciting new apps, we can be with you every step of the way.

**To find out more visit os.uk/getoutside**

# RESPECTING
# THE COUNTRYSIDE

You can't beat getting outside in the British countryside, but it's vital that we leave no trace when we're enjoying the great outdoors.

Let's make sure that generations to come can enjoy the countryside just as we do.

- Leave no trace
- Keep dogs under control; bin and bag waste
- Do not light fires; only BBQ at official sites
- Leave gates as you find them
- Keep to footpaths and open access land
- Plan ahead for your trip

For more details please visit gov.uk/countryside-code

## USING THIS GUIDE

### Easy-to-follow Suffolk and Essex Coast and Heaths walks for all

### Before setting off

**Check the walk information panel to plan your outing**

- Consider using **Public transport** where flagged. If driving, note the satnav postcode for the car park under **Parking**
- The suggested **Time** is based on a gentle pace
- Note the availability of **Cafés**, tearooms and pubs, and **Toilets**

**Terrain and hilliness**

- **Terrain** indicates the nature of the route surface
- Any rises and falls are noted under **Hilliness**

**Walking with your dog?**

- This panel states where **Dogs** must be on a lead and how many stiles there are – in case you need to lift your dog
- Keep dogs on leads where there are livestock and between April and August in forest and on grassland where there are ground-nesting birds

### A perfectly pocket-sized walking guide

- Handily sized for ease of use on each walk
- When not being read, it fits nicely into a pocket…
- …so between points, put this book in the pocket of your coat, trousers or day sack and enjoy your stroll in glorious countryside – we've made it pocket-sized for a reason!

### Flexibility of route presentation to suit all readers

- **Not comfortable map reading?** Then use the simple-to-follow route profile and accompanying route description and pictures
- **Happy to map read?** New-look walk mapping makes it easier for you to focus on the route and the points of interest along the way
- **Read the insightful Did you know?, Local legend, Stories behind the walk** and **Nature notes** to help you make the most of your day out and to enjoy all that each walk has to offer

## OS information about the walk

- Many of the features and symbols shown are taken from Ordnance Survey's celebrated **Explorer** mapping, designed to help people across Great Britain enjoy leisure time spent outside

- National Grid reference for the start point
- Explorer sheet map covering the route

**OS information**
TM 508919
Explorer OL40

## The easy-to-use walk map

- **Large-scale** mapping for ultra-clear route finding

- **Numbered points** at key turns along the route that tie in with the route instructions and respective points marked on the profile

- **Pictorial symbols** for intuitive map reading, see Map Symbols on the front cover flap

## The simple-to-follow walk profile

- Progress easily along the route using the illustrative profile, it has **numbered points** for key turning points and **graduated distance** markers

- Easy-read **route directions** with turn-by-turn detail

- Reassuring **route photographs** for each numbered point

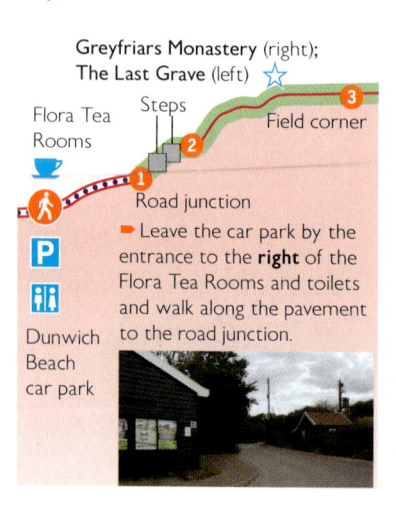

→ Leave the car park by the entrance to the **right** of the Flora Tea Rooms and toilets and walk along the pavement to the road junction.

12   Short Walks Made Easy

## Using QR codes

- Scan each QR code to see the route in Ordnance Survey's OS Maps App
*NB You may need to download a scanning app if you have an older phone*

- OS Maps will open the route automatically if you have it installed. If not, the route will open in the web version of OS Maps

- Please click **Start Route** button to begin navigating or **Download Route** to store the route for offline use

Suffolk and Essex Coast and Heaths 13

WALK 1

# OULTON BROAD

This off-road walk takes in both Oulton Broad's southern shore and the enormous Carlton Marshes Nature Reserve, a mecca for wading birds and raptors. In summer, the marshes come alive with dragonflies, while in winter look out for wigeon, snipe and teal. Although only 2 miles long, if the weather turns the route can be made briefer still via a shortcut. If you're keen to explore the area further, the visitor centre organises boat trips with knowledgeable wildlife guides.

| OS information |
| --- |
| TM 508919 Explorer OL40 |
| **Distance** 2 miles/3.2km |
| **Time** 1¼ hours |
| **Start/Finish** Carlton Marshes Nature Reserve |
| **Parking** NR33 8HU Carlton Marshes Visitor Centre car park, Burnt Hill Lane, Carlton Colville |
| **Public toilets** At the visitor centre |
| **Cafés/pubs** Visitor Centre café; Ivy House Country Hotel, passed between 2 and 3 |
| **Terrain** Grassy paths, stone track, asphalt path |
| **Hilliness** Level throughout |
| **Footwear** Winter 🥾 Spring/Summer/Autumn 👟 |

14  Short Walks Made Easy

### 🚆 Public transport

Train services to Oulton Broad South Station, 175 yards from ③: thetrainline.com

🚌 Bus service 106, Lowestoft to Burnt Hill, using Chaulkers Cresent stop on Beccles Road, ⅓ mile from 🚶: firstbus.co.uk/norfolk-suffolk

### ♿ Accessibility

Wheelchairs in and around the visitor centre and from ❽ to end; the reserve's Sprat's Water and Share Marsh trails are accessible. All-terrain pushchairs in dry conditions from 🚶 to ❹

### 🐕 Dogs

Welcome but keep on leads. No stiles

**Did you know?** On the eastern shore of Oulton Broad, outside the Lowestoft Museum (lowestoftmuseum.org), sits an old cannon on a smart new carriage built by local students. Bearing the strange name Minion Largest, it dates from the late 17th century and was once part of Lowestoft's seaward defences. During World War II, this and other local cannons suffered the indignity of being secretly buried to keep them safe.

**Local legend** In 1851, a double-crossing old salt called Captain 'Blood' Stevenson attempted to make off to the Netherlands in a wherry called *Mayfly* with £400,000 and the boat owner's daughter, Millicent. The young woman resisted Stevenson's advances, was wounded and, with her dying breath, stabbed the skipper through the heart. At Oulton Broad around 12.30am each 24 June, the phosphorescent ghost of the *Mayfly* is said to appear, accompanied by Millicent's terrified screams.

Walk 1 Oulton Broad

# STORIES BEHIND THE WALK

🐦 **Carlton Marshes** Home to 1,000 acres of open water, floodplain marsh and lowland fen, Carlton Marshes is one of the nation's more extensive nature reserves and boasts 'some of the largest populations of wading birds in the East of England'. Its modern, fully accessible visitor centre offers information on recent bird sightings, a small souvenir shop, an adventure playground for children and a café. Mobility scooters can also be hired.

☆ **George Borrow** A hugely popular author in his day — with the public rather than critics — Borrow is thought of today as one of the most original writers of the 19th century. In 1840, he moved to a small estate at Oulton Broad which belonged to his wife, Mary Clarke. A multi-linguist and inveterate traveller, his most enduring works were the fruits of his travels and, in particular, his meetings with Romany people in Europe.

---

Path crossroads — **Angles Path** — T-junction — ❶ Kissing-gate — ❷ Drive to Ivy House Country Hotel

🐦 Carlton Marshes Nature Reserve

Carlton Marshes Visitor Centre car park

▶ From the car park, head towards the visitor centre and turn **right** along a path immediately before it.
▶ At a crossroads with another path, go **straight over**, joining the Angles Way and walk to a path T-junction in 400 yards.

❶ ▶ At the T-junction, for a shorter walk, turn **left**, and rejoin the route at ❻.
▶ Otherwise, turn **right**, continuing along the Angles Way for 50 yards to a kissing-gate (left).

16  Short Walks Made Easy

## ☆ Oulton Broad

Sharing its name with the village that has grown up next to it, Oulton Broad is not the natural body of water it appears. In common with all the broads, it's a pit dug out by peat cutters – probably in medieval times – which subsequently flooded. The southernmost broad, and the only one not found in Norfolk, it's linked to the River Waveney via Oulton Dyke. Perhaps surprisingly, it's also believed to be the world's oldest motorboat racing venue (lobmbc.online).

## ☆ Lowestoft Porcelain

Operating from 1757 to 1802, the Lowestoft Porcelain Factory rode the wave of a shift in England towards gentility and a desire to show off one's wealth. It produced high-quality crockery from conveniently local white clay, cattle bones and flint (for silica). Nowadays, rare pieces can fetch thousands of pounds but you can feast your eyes on a magnificent collection for free at the nearby Lowestoft Museum (lowestoftmuseum.org).

☆ Oulton Broad

½ mile — Holiday lodge park — ❸ Stony track and bench — ❹ Tubby's Marina — 1 mile

**❷** ▶ Turn **left** and go through the gate.
▶ In 100 yards, keep **forward** across the drive to Ivy House.
▶ Carry on for ⅓ mile, walking through a holiday lodge park, crossing two drives, to emerge on a stony track by a bench.

**❸** ▶ Go **left** along the stony track. (Keeping **ahead** here leads to Oulton Broad South Station.)
▶ Reach a Tubby's Marina sign in 175 yards.

**❹** ▶ At the sign, just beyond a small car park, turn **left** to enter the marina.
▶ Follow a footpath that passes to the **left** of the marina office.
▶ Beyond the marina, walk just under ¼ mile to reach an Ivy House Country Hotel sign.

Walk 1  Oulton Broad   17

# NATURE NOTES

True to their name, marsh harriers patrol the skies above Carlton Marshes. The biggest of the harriers, in profile they make a distinct V-shape with their wings while gliding. The nature reserve also provides a haven for a much smaller but no less deadly aerial hunter: the dragonfly. No fewer than 28 species have been recorded here.

Fields and wetlands provide a favourable habitat for lapwings, while hedgerows are home to yellowhammers – once common farmland birds for which Carlton Marshes is a sanctuary.

In early summer, you'll see marsh marigolds – a member of the buttercup family – turning the marshes a striking yellow.

You'll also pass plants that enjoy waterside locations such as cattail and hemp agrimony, the latter being extremely attractive to butterflies and used as an anti-inflammatory agent in traditional medicine.

Look out too for field briars (a species of wild rose), purple loosestrife, tufted vetch and the large snow-white flowers of hedge bindweed.

Lapwing

Carlton Marshes sign

**Oulton Broad**

Ivy House Country Hotel sign

Carlton

**5** ➤ At the hotel sign, bear sharp **right**, ignoring another path immediately to your left signed to Ivy House.
➤ Later, ignore a path off left as your path swings **right** in 400 yards, and continue to a Carlton Marshes sign.

**6** ➤ At the sign, unless you wish to take a shortcut back to the visitor centre, ignore a path off to your left and continue **ahead** on a grassy path.
➤ This leads to a set of steps, left, in ⅓ mile.

18  Short Walks Made Easy

**Above:** marsh harrier
**Below:** marsh marigold (left), mallow (right)

**Top:** cattail
**Above:** yellowhammer

**7** ▶ Turn **left** down eight steps and go **forward** to a gate.
▶ Pass through the gate and follow the path as it bears **left** through marshland to a kissing-gate.

**8** ▶ Go through the gate to turn **left** along a broad crushed-stone track and walk to a path crossroads in 175 yards.

**9** ▶ At the path crossroads, by a signpost for the visitor centre, turn **right**. The car park will soon appear on your **left**.

Walk 1 Oulton Broad  19

# WALK 2

## SOUTHWOLD

The favourite holiday destination of former Prime Minister Gordon Brown, Southwold is a genteel, pleasingly old-fashioned resort. Perhaps surprisingly, it was once the home to the godfather of dystopian fiction, George Orwell. You can enjoy the Orwell mural at the wonderful pier where this walk begins, before heading along the prom and the dunes to the mouth of the River Blyth, with its famous rowing-boat ferry. Skirting a coastal marshland, you'll return through the heart of this beguiling town.

**CATCH A BUS**

### OS information

TM 511767
Explorer 231

**Distance**
3.1 miles/5km

**Time**
1¾ hours

**Start/Finish**
Southwold Pier

**Parking** IP18 6BN
Southwold Pier car park, North Parade

**Public toilets**
In the car park; near Alfred Corry Lifeboat Museum at ❷

**Cafés/pubs**
Southwold

**Terrain**
Pavement, grassy path; sandy beach (optional)

**Hilliness**
Level throughout

**Footwear**
Year round

**Public transport**
Bus services 99, Lowestoft to Southwold; 99A, Halesworth and Bungay to Southwold; 146, Norwich to Southwold; bus stop on A1095, opposite Pier Avenue: firstbus.co.uk/norfolk-suffolk; border-bus.co.uk

20   Short Walks Made Easy

### Accessibility

Wheelchair and pushchair friendly on the Southwold sections, from 🚶 to ① and ④ to end

### Dogs

Welcome but keep on leads. No stiles

**Local legend** A very curious experience befell one Arthur Slater CBE on the evening of 1 February 1976. Heading home from church across Southwold's South Green, he came across two phantom leafless thorn hedges. He described the apparitions as 'waist high and covered in raindrops' and stretching 'about 40 yards'. Slater struck one with his walking stick and felt 'slight resistance' but when he tried to grasp it, his hand went straight through. The hedges disappeared soon after.

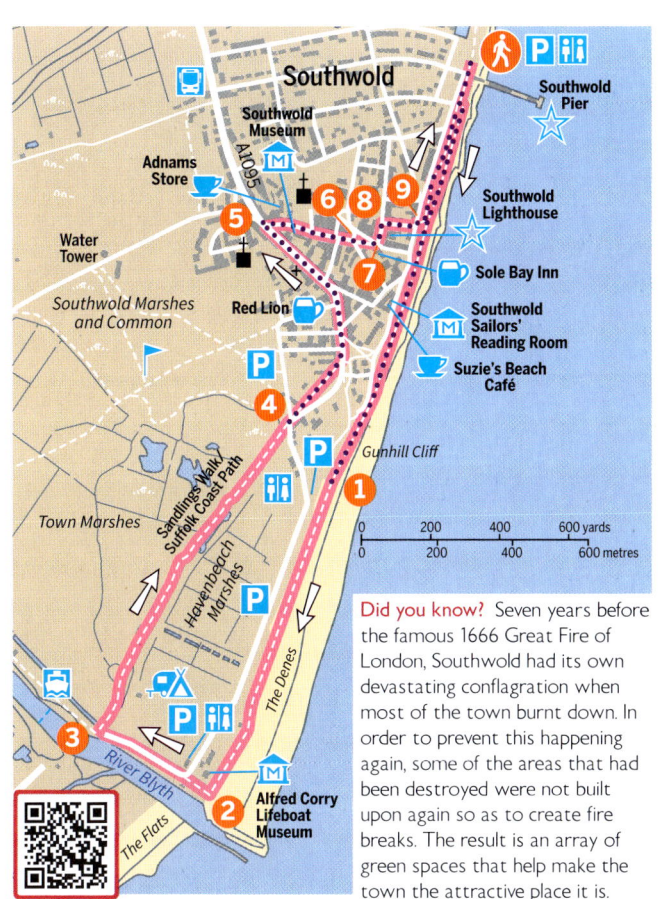

**Did you know?** Seven years before the famous 1666 Great Fire of London, Southwold had its own devastating conflagration when most of the town burnt down. In order to prevent this happening again, some of the areas that had been destroyed were not built upon again so as to create fire breaks. The result is an array of green spaces that help make the town the attractive place it is.

Walk 2 Southwold  21

# STORIES BEHIND THE WALK

⭐ **Southwold Pier** Opened in 1900, Southwold Pier stretched 810 feet into the sea before a series of unfortunate events – a storm, World War II invasion preparations, a loose mine, and two more storms – reduced it to a mere 60 feet. Today, the elegant pier runs to ten times that and is renowned for a collection of eccentric machines created by Tim Hunkin. Slip a pound in the slot and you can rent a dog, take a holiday in an armchair and much more (underthepier.com).

**Southwold Sailors' Reading Room** Those who built the reading room in 1864 certainly conformed to the ideas we have today of Victorian high-mindedness. The intention was to provide fishermen and mariners with a refuge that wasn't a pub and which would set them on the path of righteousness. Today there are still some reading materials scattered about, while the walls are lined with fascinating maritime photos and paraphernalia, including brightly coloured figureheads and exquisitely crafted model ships and boats (southwoldsailors readingroom.co.uk).

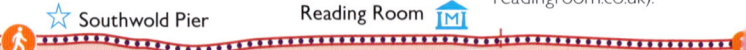

⭐ Southwold Pier

Southwold Sailors' Reading Room

Suzie's Beach Café ☕ ½ mile

Promenade

**Southwold Pier car park**

▪ From the Southwold Pier entrance, with the sea on your left, walk to the end of the promenade in ¾ mile.

▪ Just over halfway along, to visit the Southwold Sailors' Reading Room, climb steps to the **right** of Suzie's Beach Café.

**1** ▪ At the very end of the promenade, continue **ahead** through the dunes and follow any of the paths that run along them. If you prefer, walk along the sandy beach.

▪ Reach the lifeboat museum in ½ mile.

22  Short Walks Made Easy

## ☆ Southwold Lighthouse

It may be 100 feet high and vital to the safe navigation of this stretch of the North Sea, but tucked away on a side street as if it were just another dwelling, Southwold Lighthouse does look a little incongruous. Commissioned in 1890, its oil lamp caused a fire after just six days. Happily, it's long since been electrified. For those keen to take on the 113 steps, bookable tours are available (adnams.co.uk).

## Alfred Corry Lifeboat Museum

As lifeboats go, the *Alfred Corry* has had something of a multi-storied life. Commissioned in 1892 and named after an RNLI benefactor, the lifeboat served Southwold until 1918. She was sold on and renamed several times, eventually winding up in Maldon (Walk 10) where she became a houseboat called *Thorfinn*. Tracked down by a man named John 'Wiggy' Goldsmith, she was purchased and restored to her original condition and now has her own museum (alfredcorry.co.uk).

---

Dunes and sandy beach — 1 mile — Alfred Corry Lifeboat Museum ❷ — 1½ miles — River Blyth (left); caravan park (right) ❸

**❷** ▶ When you reach the small car park at the Alfred Corry Lifeboat Museum, just before the River Blyth, turn **right** to walk beside a road.

▶ Stroll to a Sandlings Walk post in 350 yards, just beyond a caravan park.

**❸** ▶ At the marker post, signed Sandlings Walk/Suffolk Coast Path, turn **right** onto a footpath. Walk for just over ½ mile to meet a road junction.

▶ The curious 'War of the Worlds' building across the marshes (left) is a water tower and famous Southwold landmark.

**Walk 2** Southwold

# NATURE NOTES

Tall dark-blue spikes of viper's bugloss dominate the rough ground above the beach in summer. A little further along, the dunes offer an excellent opportunity to see plants that tolerate sandy soils. Marram grass is the most prevalent species here. Large bushes of sea buckthorn grow above head height on the landward side of the dunes. Colourful lupins dot themselves around the landscape; yarrow gives its bright white firework display a few inches above a carpet of common restharrow, a tough and determined member of the pea family with small pink flowers.

The Southwold Marshes and Common covers a full 337 acres reclaimed from the River Blyth.

You may see cattle grazing on grasses and plants that can survive in saline conditions.

If you are tempted by any of the promenade cafés, be on your guard against herring gulls looking for an easy meal.

Sandlings Walk / Suffolk Coast Path

**4** ▶ At the junction, **cross** Gardner Road and keep **ahead** up Constitution Hill. Bear **left** at the top into Queen Street.
▶ Pass the Red Lion and at the Town Pump keep **left** into High Street. Carry on for 250 yards to Victoria Street.

**5** ▶ Go **right** onto Victoria Street, passing the Adnams Store (café, left) and Southwold Museum (right).
▶ Continue to a crossroads by the Adnams Brewery in 150 yards.

**6** ▶ At the crossroads, go **straight over** to pass a small triangular green to reach the Sole Bay Inn (left).

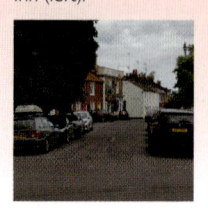

24  Short Walks Made Easy

Above: viper's bugloss
Right: common restharrow
Far right: sea buckthorn
Opposite: herring gull

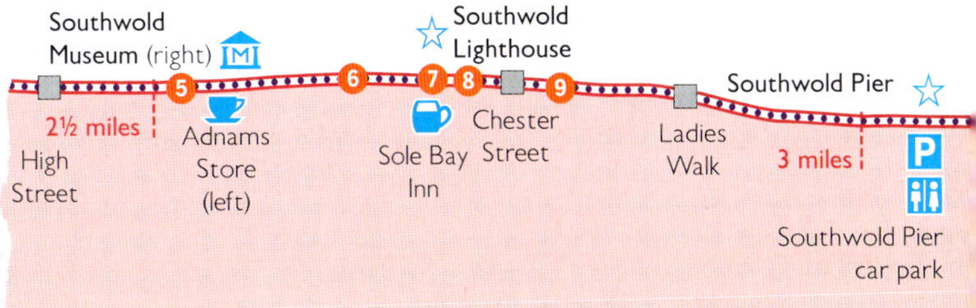

**7** ▸ Turn **left** immediately after the inn along Stradbroke Road, passing the lighthouse.

**8** ▸ Turn first **right** along Chester Road and walk to the seafront T-junction.

**9** ▸ At the junction, cross the road and turn **left** along Ladies Walk to head back to the pier.

Walk 2 Southwold

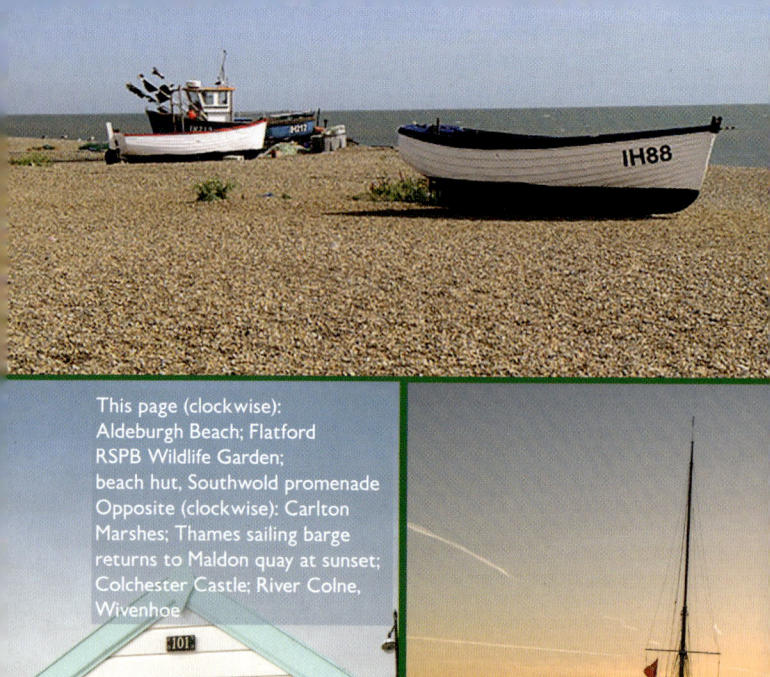

This page (clockwise):
Aldeburgh Beach; Flatford RSPB Wildlife Garden; beach hut, Southwold promenade
Opposite (clockwise): Carlton Marshes; Thames sailing barge returns to Maldon quay at sunset; Colchester Castle; River Colne, Wivenhoe

27

# WALK 3

# DUNWICH

Though most of Dunwich's history lies beneath the waves, it remains a fascinating corner of Suffolk. This route leads you from the beach to one of the final reminders of the former city's medieval glory, Greyfriars Monastery. While Greyfriars Wood was probably planted in the early 19th century, the pleasant open farmland you'll be walking through is likely to be of more ancient origin. There's a visit to the rare Leper Chapel and at the end a cosy inn – The Ship – awaits.

## OS information

TM 479707
Explorer 231

**Distance**
3.4 miles/5.4km

**Time**
2 hours

**Start/Finish**
Dunwich

**Parking** IP17 3EN
Dunwich Beach car park, Beach Road

**Public toilets**
In the car park

**Cafés/pubs**
Flora Tea Rooms at 🚶; The Ship, near ①

**Terrain**
Tarmac, grassy and woodland paths; farm track; sandy bridleway

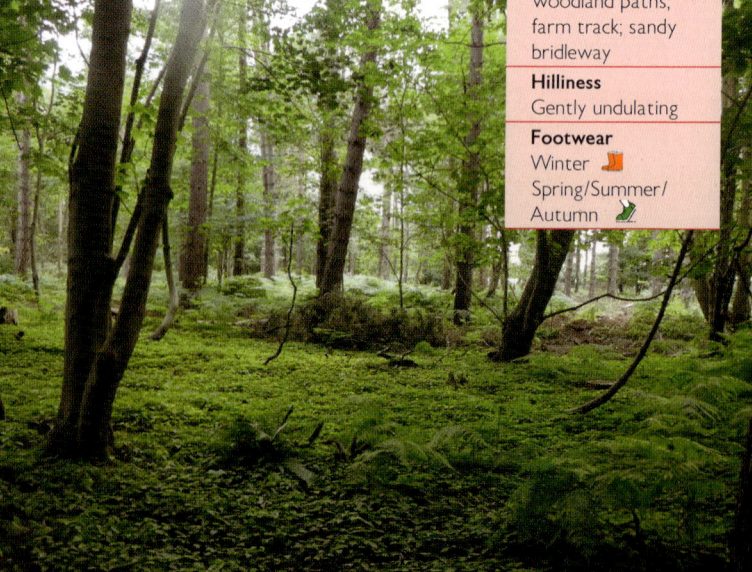

**Hilliness**
Gently undulating

**Footwear**
Winter 🥾
Spring/Summer/Autumn 👟

28  Short Walks Made Easy

**Public transport**
None

**Accessibility**
Around the village for wheelchairs and pushchairs

**Dogs**
A good dog walk. No stiles

*Did you know?* To the left of the path, just before you reach the friary (2 to 3), is a sign marking 'The Last Grave'. The grave in question belongs to Jacob Forster who died in 1796, aged 38. It's the surviving grave from the churchyard of All Saints, a church that fell into the sea in 1919. Somewhat ghoulishly, bones from other graves lost to coastal erosion emerge occasionally from the weather-beaten cliff.

*Local legend* Although it's sometimes falsely claimed that Dunwich became so large (page 30) that it boasted a church for every week of the year, we do know that at one point it had 19 places of worship, the last of which was All Saints. According to the locals, the city's church bells can still be heard – simply listen out on stormy nights to hear them chiming away from beneath the waves that claimed them.

Walk 3 Dunwich 29

# STORIES BEHIND THE WALK

☆ **The city that fell into the sea** Medieval Dunwich grew to the size of the city of London and was home to between five and six thousand inhabitants, happily prosperous on earnings from fishing, shipbuilding and trade. However, it was also exposed to terrible storms that blew in from the North Sea. In the 13th and 14th centuries, flood after flood smashed into Dunwich, changing the coastline and ripping the town into the sea, until almost nothing of it was left (see also page 29).

☆ **Greyfriars Monastery** Dunwich's first Franciscan monastery lasted but a few decades before being destroyed by the sea in a terrible storm in 1286. This second construction was wisely established further inland. However, by the time Henry VIII ordered its closure in 1539, there were only a few friars left. Sadly, their mammoth church – over 500 feet long – has disappeared. The fragments of walls that remain are thought to be part of the refectory (dunwichgreyfriars.org.uk).

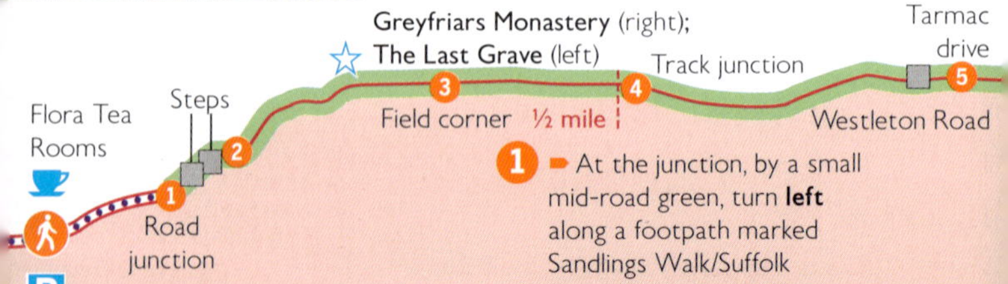

❶ ➥ At the junction, by a small mid-road green, turn **left** along a footpath marked Sandlings Walk/Suffolk Coast Path; shortly after, climb seven steps.

➥ Leave the car park by the entrance to the **right** of the Flora Tea Rooms and toilets and walk along the pavement to the road junction.

➥ After about 30 yards, turn **right** down six steps, still following the two trails, and immediately turn **left**.

30  Short Walks Made Easy

## Dunwich Museum

Your portal into the lost world of Dunwich, this compact museum imaginatively tells the story of the city that was lost to the sea. Priding itself on its packed calendar of events and activities, you could find yourself in a felt workshop, or making a pilgrim charm, or perhaps heading out on a walk with a local expert, so do check their website for details before you go (dunwichmuseum.org.uk).

## ✝ St James's Church and Leper Chapel

Tucked behind St James's Church you'll find the extensive ruins of a very unusual building. Constructed in 1206, the Leper Chapel was part of a hospital where those unfortunate enough to contract leprosy, a contagious disease, were kept in isolation from society. The hospital was built so that bedridden patients could still see inside the chapel when services were held. This would have been a kindness to those whose only real hope lay in an afterlife.

---

1 mile | **Sandlings Walk/ Suffolk Coast Path** — ❻ Minsmere Road — 1½ miles — ❼ Path crossroads

❷ ▶ After 200 yards, you'll come to Greyfriars Monastery (right), and The Last Grave (left). After visiting, continue along the footpath for 100 yards to reach a field corner.

❸ ▶ At the corner, turn **right** along a path with the friary wall to your left.
▶ Remain on the path as it goes **left**, passing through the wall into Greyfriars Wood.
▶ Carry on through the wood for 200 yards to a track junction.

**Walk 3** Dunwich

# NATURE NOTES

Undoubtedly the most spectacular time to visit Greyfriars Wood is in the summer when it comes alive with foxgloves. On account of their heart-shaped fruit, this (poisonous) plant was employed by medieval apothecaries to treat heart problems. Curiously, they were right to do so, because foxgloves contain digitalin which is used today for certain heart conditions (though produced synthetically nowadays).

The mixed woodland contains a range of mostly native trees. See if you can spot the graceful ash, the spiky leaves of holly and the generous elder, which provides us with both elderflowers for wines and cordials, and elderberries full of anti-oxidants, which are excellent for treating colds. Meanwhile, sweet-smelling honeysuckle climbs in and over the bramble, immune to its thorns. Out beyond the wood's fringes, look downwards along the path edges for greater plantain. These plants are often the first to colonise disturbed ground, and they can withstand a degree of trampling, so can typically be found along footpaths.

*Holly berries*

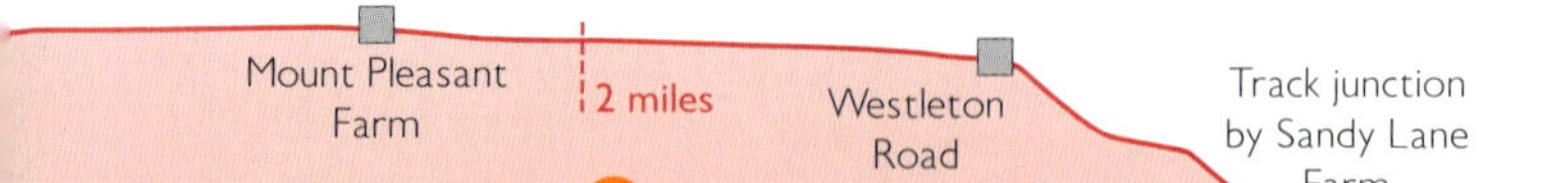

**4** ▬ At the junction, turn **right**, following the Sandlings Walk/ Suffolk Coast Path sign after an information board.
▬ When the track meets a road, continue **ahead** for 150 yards to a tarmac drive (left).

**5** ▬ Turn **left** along the drive, following a Sandlings Walk/ Suffolk Coast Path sign. The drive becomes a footpath after passing a pair of houses.
▬ Keep **ahead** after a gate, ignoring all side paths to reach a road.

**6** ▬ **Cross** Minsmere Road and continue along a sandy bridleway to reach a path crossing in ⅓ mile.

Mount Pleasant Farm — 2 miles — Westleton Road — Track junction by Sandy Lane Farm **8** — 2½ miles

32  Short Walks Made Easy

**Top left**: honeysuckle
**Above**: unripened elderberries
**Left**: foxgloves
**Below**: plantain

## ☆ Dunwich: the city that fell into the sea

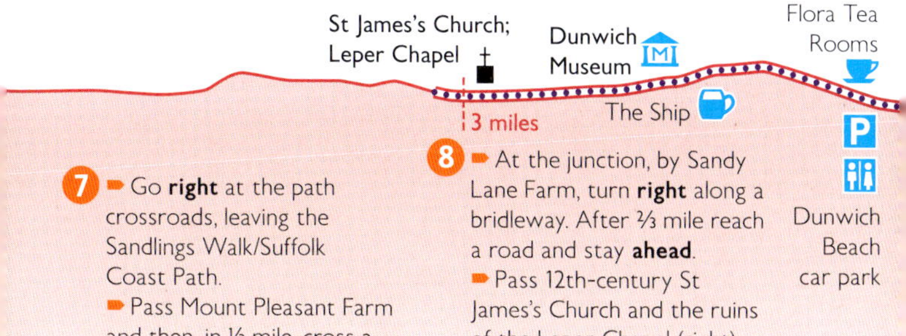

St James's Church; Leper Chapel
Dunwich Museum
Flora Tea Rooms
The Ship
Dunwich Beach car park

3 miles

**7** ➤ Go **right** at the path crossroads, leaving the Sandlings Walk/Suffolk Coast Path.
➤ Pass Mount Pleasant Farm and then, in ⅓ mile, cross a road to keep **ahead** for ¼ mile to a track T-junction.

**8** ➤ At the junction, by Sandy Lane Farm, turn **right** along a bridleway. After ⅔ mile reach a road and stay **ahead**.
➤ Pass 12th-century St James's Church and the ruins of the Leper Chapel (right).
➤ Follow the road to **1** and go left into Dunwich.

Walk 3 Dunwich  33

WALK 4

CATCH A BUS

# ALDEBURGH AND THE RIVER ALDE

An important port in the Middle Ages, Aldeburgh is a resort full of interesting and often quirky buildings. However, this route does not confine itself to the town but also heads out along the coast for a circuit of Aldeburgh Marshes, mostly via an embankment alongside the peaceful River Alde. The route visits Aldeburgh Museum in the medieval Moot Hall, passes a lookout tower that has become an arts hub, and descends the resort's historic Town Steps.

| OS information |
|---|
| TM 465568 Explorer 212 |
| **Distance** 4 miles / 6.5 km |
| **Time** 2¼ hours |
| **Start/Finish** Aldeburgh |
| **Parking** IP15 5DE Fort Green car park, Slaughden Road |
| **Public toilets** In the car park; opposite the Moot Hall, 9 |
| **Cafés/pubs** Aldeburgh |
| **Terrain** Promenade, pavement and tarmac path; stony road; grassy embankment; grassy paths, marshy after prolonged rain |
| **Hilliness** Level throughout except for one descent of 46 steps (leading to 8) |
| **Footwear** Spring/Autumn/Winter 🥾 Summer 👟 |

34   Short Walks Made Easy

## Public transport

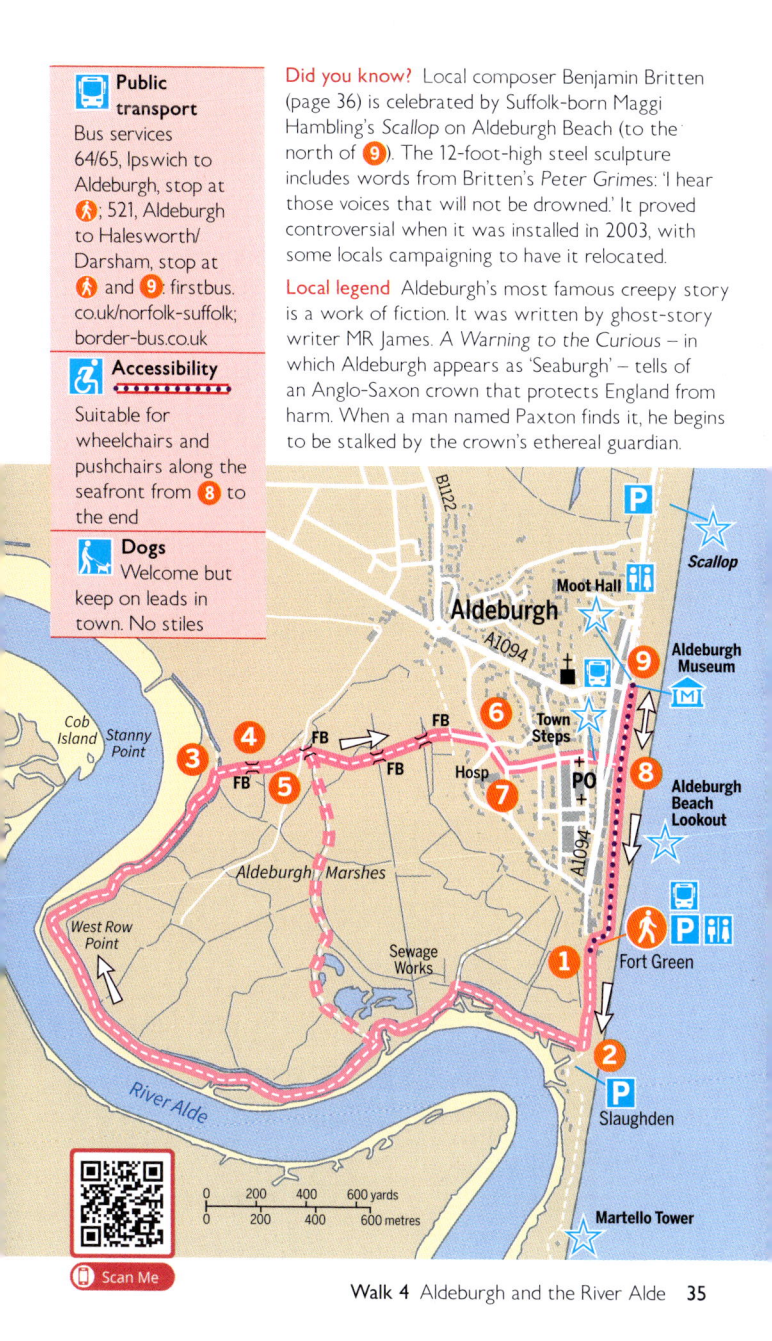

Bus services 64/65, Ipswich to Aldeburgh, stop at (8); 521, Aldeburgh to Halesworth/Darsham, stop at (8) and (9); firstbus.co.uk/norfolk-suffolk; border-bus.co.uk

## Accessibility

Suitable for wheelchairs and pushchairs along the seafront from (8) to the end

## Dogs

Welcome but keep on leads in town. No stiles

**Did you know?** Local composer Benjamin Britten (page 36) is celebrated by Suffolk-born Maggi Hambling's *Scallop* on Aldeburgh Beach (to the north of (9)). The 12-foot-high steel sculpture includes words from Britten's *Peter Grimes*: 'I hear those voices that will not be drowned.' It proved controversial when it was installed in 2003, with some locals campaigning to have it relocated.

**Local legend** Aldeburgh's most famous creepy story is a work of fiction. It was written by ghost-story writer MR James. *A Warning to the Curious* – in which Aldeburgh appears as 'Seaburgh' – tells of an Anglo-Saxon crown that protects England from harm. When a man named Paxton finds it, he begins to be stalked by the crown's ethereal guardian.

**Walk 4** Aldeburgh and the River Alde  35

# STORIES BEHIND THE WALK

☆ **Benjamin Britten and Peter Pears** In his lifetime, Suffolk-born Benjamin Britten became one of the most significant British composers of the 20th century. One of his best-loved operas, *Peter Grimes*, is set in Aldeburgh, where he and his partner, Peter Pears, lived for the last 19 years of Britten's life. Pears, a professional tenor, worked closely with Britten and appeared in most of his 15 operas.

☆ **Martello Tower** In the early 19th century, rumours of an imminent invasion by Napoleon were on everyone's lips. To ward off the French army, a string of Martello Towers was built along England's southern and eastern coast; the one at Slaughden is the country's largest. It was started in 1806, the year after Nelson's important but far from war-ending victory at Trafalgar. However, after six years of construction and the use of millions of bricks, the tower was abandoned.

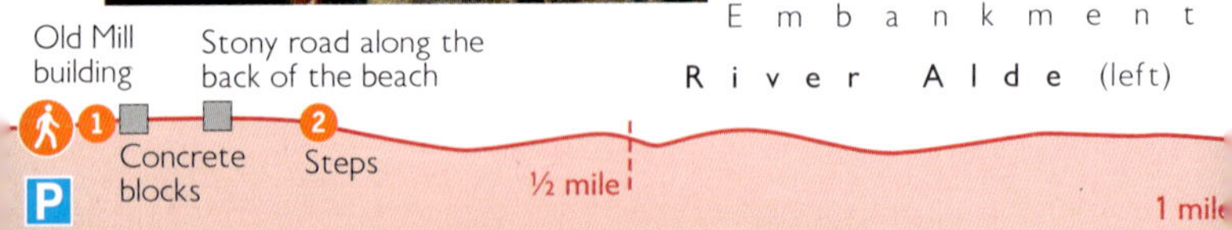

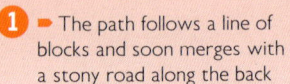

Embankment

River Alde (left)

Old Mill building | Stony road along the back of the beach
Concrete blocks | Steps ② | ½ mile | 1 mile

Fort Green car park

① ▶ The path follows a line of blocks and soon merges with a stony road along the back of the beach.
▶ Keep **ahead**, sea on your left. In 250 yards, turn **right** down six steps and head along the path immediately opposite.

▶ Begin with the sea on your left. Head through the car park to the **right** of the Old Mill building and then leave it via a footpath between concrete blocks.

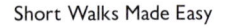

36  Short Walks Made Easy

☆ **Aldeburgh Beach Lookout** There was once a time when towers like this were numerous along the Suffolk coast. Men would stand at the top looking out for distress signals from passing ships then shout down to pilots who would row out and attempt to save or salvage them. This tower was bought by Caroline Wiseman and her late partner Francis Carnwath around 2010 and has been turned into a hub of artistic creativity that's well worth visiting (aldeburghbeachlookout. com).

🏛 **Aldeburgh Museum** Set in a rather fetching 16th-century Moot Hall (the town's former assembly rooms), the museum has undergone a transformation in recent years bringing it firmly into the 21st century. It offers a range of hands-on displays and state-of-the-art digital media to guide visitors through the history of the town and its people from Anglo-Saxon times to the present (aldeburghmuseum.org.uk).

f o o t p a t h

R i v e r   A l d e  (left)

1½ miles         2 miles

❷ ▶ Continue along an embankment for 2 miles through various gates, the River Alde on your left, to a flight of steps (right).
▶ (After ½ mile, at the second footpath on the right, there's a shortcut across the marshes; you can rejoin the route at a footbridge after ❺).

❸ ▶ At the steps, head **down** off the embankment and follow a path as it goes through a gate and hugs the left-hand hedge along a field, aiming for a corner in 150 yards.

**Walk 4** Aldeburgh and the River Alde 37

# NATURE NOTES

The herring gull's cry is one of the most evocative sounds of the British seaside. Here you'll find the gull mixing with the smaller and rather misnamed black-headed gulls – in summer their heads are chocolate brown while in winter their heads turn white with a grey spot on the side.

On the beach you'll find three large and easily identifiable plants: sea kale is the coastal version of the kale family (and is a protected species so don't be tempted to harvest a leaf); red valerian is adept at thriving on next to nothing; while hollyhocks are doubtless escapees from gardens in the town.

Aldeburgh Marshes, criss-crossed by dykes, and the River Alde provide a welcoming habitat for mute swans and geese. The wetlands are fringed by wild carrot, also known as Queen Anne's lace. The plants do smell of carrot but their roots do not develop the familiar garden vegetable.

Sea kale

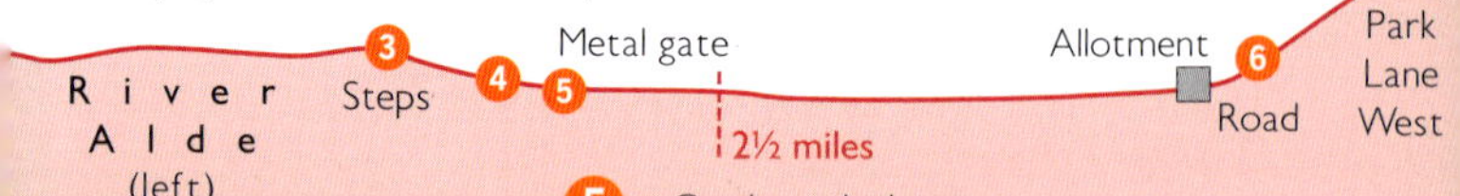

**5** ▶ Go through the small gate (right of a larger one) and bear sharp **left** towards another gate.
▶ **Cross** a footbridge and bear **right** along the path across the marsh, going from gate to gate.
▶ After ½ mile, pass through an allotment and on by tennis courts to a road.

**4** ▶ Before reaching the corner though, bear **right** to cut across to a metal gate. Ignore the metal gates to your left.

**6** ▶ Turn **right** along the road for 150 yards to the second turning on the left, opposite an ornate brick water tower.

38  Short Walks Made Easy

**Above**: hollyhock
**Below**: red valerian

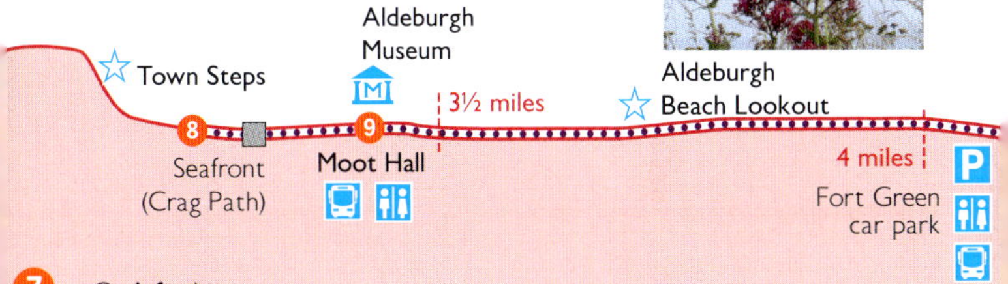

**Top**: black-headed gull   **Bottom**: wild carrot

Town Steps

Aldeburgh Museum

3½ miles

Aldeburgh Beach Lookout

**8** Seafront (Crag Path)

**9** Moot Hall

4 miles

Fort Green car park

**7** ▶ Go **left** along Park Lane West. Keep **ahead** at a crossroads and carry on to the Town Steps at the end of Park Lane.

▶ After enjoying the view, descend the 46 steps. Carry **straight on** across two more roads to reach the seafront.

**8** ▶ Turn **left** along the seafront road (Crag Path) to reach the historic Moot Hall (and Aldeburgh Museum) in 300 yards.

▶ To see *Scallop*, detour ⅓ mile each way, up and back along the seafront.

**9** ▶ Otherwise, put the sea on your left and walk south along the promenade. Keep **forward** when this becomes a road (Crag Path), pass the South Lookout, and then in 350 yards arrive back at Fort Green car park.

**Walk 4** Aldeburgh and the River Alde   39

Opposite (clockwise): dunlin; cattle grazing Carlton Marshes; sweet chestnuts; comfrey
This page (clockwise): mallow; forget-me-nots; herring gull

40

41

# WALK 5

# ORFORD AND THE RIVER ORE

In common with Dunwich (page 28), Orford was a major port that was undone by the action of the sea, although in quite a different way (page 44). Today it's a picturesque village of winsome cottages and the multiple-award-winning Pump Street Bakery, and is, understandably, popular with tourists. This walk takes you out of the hubbub to a peaceful stretch of gorgeous riverside, with views of Orford Ness and its enormous transmission towers, ending with a stop at a unique castle built by Henry II.

| OS information |
|---|
| TM 425496 Explorer 212 |

| **Distance** |
|---|
| 3.5 miles/5.7km |
| **Time** |
| 2 hours |
| **Start/Finish** |
| Orford |
| **Parking** IP12 2NU |
| Quay Street car park |
| **Public toilets** |
| In the car park |
| **Cafés/pubs** |
| Orford |
| **Terrain** |
| Grassy paths, lane and sandy track |
| **Hilliness** |
| Mostly level, with a short rise ④ to ⑤ and descent from ⑧ |

42  Short Walks Made Easy

**Footwear**
Winter 🥾
Spring/Summer/
Autumn 🥾

**Public transport**
None

**Accessibility**
••••••••••
Wheelchairs and pushchairs around the village and down to the Quay

**Dogs**
A good dog walk. No stiles

**Did you know?** Although most of the locations for Mackenzie Crook's hit television comedy series *Detectorists* can be found in Framlingham in Suffolk, Orford featured in several episodes as well. The village primary school was used as the workplace for the long-suffering Becky (played by Rachael Stirling), while The Kings Head Inn had a small role in the first series.

**Local legend** Early in the history of Orford Castle, its residents were brought a very strange offering: some fisherman had caught in their nets a sort of merman. He was covered with hair apart from a bald head, and spoke no language beyond a few guttural noises. Held in the castle for a while, the 'Wild Man of Orford' appeared content, but during one of the sea swims his captors allowed him, he simply swam away and disappeared forever.

Walk 5  Orford and the River Ore

# STORIES BEHIND THE WALK

☆ **Orford Ness** Orford was once a significant port. However, North Sea currents moved sediment along the coast – a process called longshore drift – causing the shingle spit of Orford Ness to grow, and making Orford's harbour increasingly inaccessible. Nowadays, the spit stretches all the way from Aldeburgh to several miles south-west of Orford. Understandably, ship captains began opting for ports with simpler access and Orford's days as a thriving port came to an end.

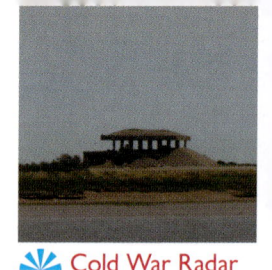

**Cold War Radar Station** In the late 1960s, the US military built an 'over-the-horizon' radar station at Orford Ness to improve its spying capabilities in Eastern Europe. However, this 'Cobra Mist' project was short lived due to unexplained problems with noise, and the station closed in 1973. It was replaced by a transmitting station run by the Foreign Office, then the BBC World Service and finally by Radio Caroline. Of the 12 towers still standing, five are 340 feet tall.

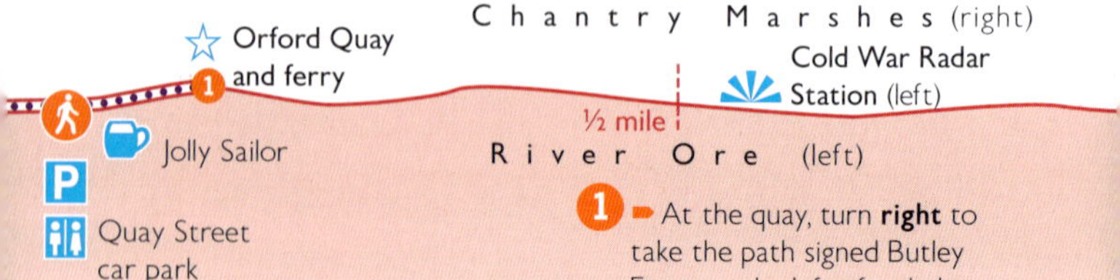

Chantry Marshes (right)

☆ Orford Quay and ferry

Cold War Radar Station (left)

Jolly Sailor

½ mile

River Ore (left)

Quay Street car park

❶ ▸ At the quay, turn **right** to take the path signed Butley Ferry to the left of a shelter.
▸ Walk beside the River Ore for almost 1½ miles to a marker post. On the way, after 400 yards, look left to make out the radar towers.

▸ Leave the car park at the entrance and turn **left** down the road to Orford Quay.

44  Short Walks Made Easy

## ⭐ Orford Quay and ferry

The modest quay at Orford is a far cry from the bustling harbour of old but it serves day-trippers very well. There are breakfast, lunch and dinner cruises on offer, and circumnavigations of Havergate Island, an important RSPB reserve. The National Trust runs a ferry service to visit the National Nature Reserve and former radar station at Orford Ness. However, tickets are limited and sell out quickly so do check the website and book (nationaltrust.org.uk).

## 🏰 Orford Castle

Built by Henry II between 1265 and 1273 as a counter to the power of Hugh Bigod, Earl of Norfolk, Orford's octagonal keep is unique in Britain. Captured briefly by the French in 1215, it led an otherwise largely untroubled life until its fortunes waned with those of Orford. The castle owes its continued existence to the fact that it served as a useful landmark to 19th-century sailors and was thus deemed worth preserving (english-heritage.org.uk).

Chantry Point | Chantry Marshes (right) | 1 mile | 1½ miles | Marker post ②

River Ore (left)

**②** ▶ At the marker post, head down off the embankment and inland to a lane in ½ mile.

**③** ▶ Turn **right** along the lane for almost ¼ mile to the point where it begins to bend right, by Richmond Farm.

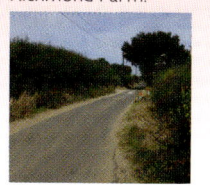

**④** ▶ As the road starts to bend right, at a footpath fingerpost on the left, turn **left** along a wide sandy track. In just under 100 yards, reach a footpath and fingerpost on the right.

Walk 5 Orford and the River Ore   45

# NATURE NOTES

The glorious Chantry Marshes to the west of Orford offer a largely undisturbed habitat for insects such as the meadow brown butterfly. As you stride alongside the River Ore, keep an eye out for foraging redshanks. As their name suggests, these waders have bright red legs. Sea lavender and mallow grow on the embankment.

On the farmland behind the marsh, the summer hedgerows are enlivened by two brassicas: black mustard has little yellow flowers and was a popular condiment in Roman times, while garlic mustard – often known as Jack by the hedge – has been used as a spice for millennia. Come the autumn, the blackthorn hedges will produce dusky blue berries for making sloe gin, while the fruit of the sweet chestnut trees lie about for anyone happy to risk having their fingers pricked.

**5** ▸ At the fingerpost, go **right**, up five steps. Follow the footpath as it crosses three fields in a straight line, directly towards Orford Castle, until you reach a driveway.

**6** ▸ Head **straight across** the driveway and follow the signed footpath, passing through a wood and over an open grassy area to reach the castle car park.

46 Short Walks Made Easy

Above: redshank
Left: black mustard
Right: Jack by the hedge
**Opposite page**:
blackthorn or sloe berries

**7** ▶ After visiting the castle, return to the car park and turn **left** up Castle Hill.
▶ Follow the road round to the **right**, pass The Crown and Castle, and head across a market square to a road junction, the church ahead/left.

**8** ▶ Keep **straight on** along Market Hill (church over to the left).
▶ The road bends sharp **right** (take care as there is no pavement on the corner).
▶ Keep **ahead** down Church Street then Quay Street to return to the car park.

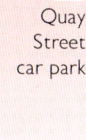

Walk 5 Orford and the River Ore  47

# WALK 6

## SUTTON HOO

Sutton Hoo burst into the limelight in 1939 when archaeologists announced the discovery of a royal Anglo-Saxon ship burial there. This walk takes advantage of the public footpaths that cross the famous 255-acre estate, which is owned nowadays by the National Trust. The route takes in views of the marina at Woodbridge and the River Deben, and looks over Mound 2, the largest of the impressive tumuli that make up the Royal Burial Ground.

**CATCH A BUS**

### OS information
TM 290493
Explorer 197

**Distance**
2.9 miles/4.6km

**Time**
1¾ hours

**Start/Finish**
Sutton Hoo

**Parking** IP12 3DJ
National Trust car park

**Public toilets**
Sutton Hoo (on purchase of ticket)

**Cafés/pubs**
National Trust café

**Terrain**
Driveways; stony and grassy paths

**Hilliness**
Lengthy but gentle descents and ascents

**Footwear**
Year round

**Public transport**
Bus service 70, Ipswich to Woodbridge via Melton Station, with stop at Sutton Hoo entrance, 1 mile from Melton Station: firstbus.co.uk/norfolk-suffolk

**Accessibility**
Suitable for powered wheelchairs and all-terrain pushchairs from 🚶 to ④ and ⑤ to end.

**Dogs** Welcome but keep on leads. No stiles

**Did you know?** John Preston wrote a novel, *The Dig*, based on events at Sutton Hoo in 1938–39. The author was the nephew of Margaret Guido, one of the archaeologists involved in the excavation. While the novel is broadly factual, Preston allowed himself some licence in describing what happened. In 2021, *The Dig* was made into a feature film of the same name starring Carey Mulligan as Edith Pretty and Suffolk-born Ralph Fiennes as Basil Brown.

**Local legend** Three separate and quite different supernatural phenomena encouraged Edith Pretty to excavate her estate's Anglo-Saxon burial mounds. She had a dream about the burial of a helmeted horse-rider along with various golden items. A medium called William Parish held a séance during which a mounted soldier instructed her to investigate the mounds. And a friend, Dorothy Cox, saw the ghosts of Anglo-Saxon soldiers every time she visited. What choice did Edith have?

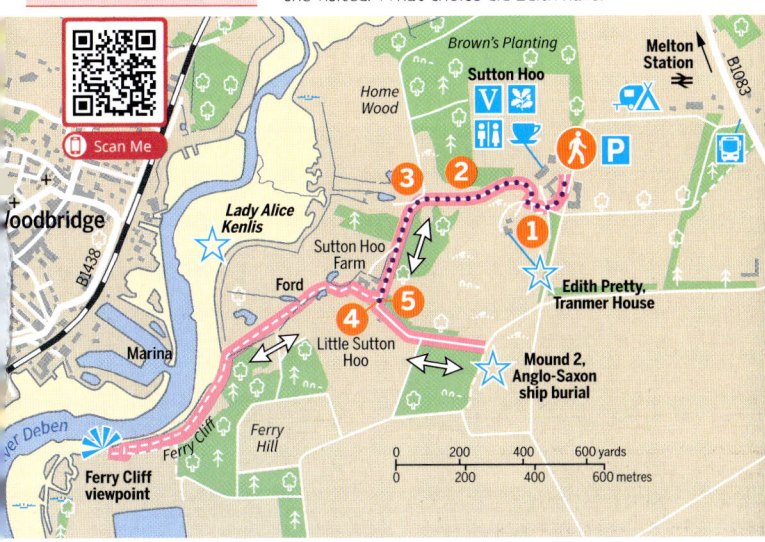

Walk 6 Sutton Hoo    49

# STORIES BEHIND THE WALK

### 🌿 Sutton Hoo

'Hoo' means 'spur of land' in Old English and, in the case of Sutton Hoo, describes the ground offering a vantage point above the River Deben. It's no surprise that the location – conveniently situated above a river whence a ship could be dragged with relative ease – would suggest itself as a last resting place for royalty. And perhaps there are more secrets still to come. In 2000, a second burial ground was discovered on a second 'hoo' about 500 yards upstream.

### ☆ Edith Pretty

When Edith Pretty purchased Tranmer House in 1926, it was taken as read that, over the centuries, looters had spirited away anything of value from the burial mounds on the estate. Had it not been for her determination to follow the supernatural guidance she was convinced she'd received (page 49), it's quite possible that the astonishing finds at Sutton Hoo might even today be mouldering beneath the Suffolk turf.

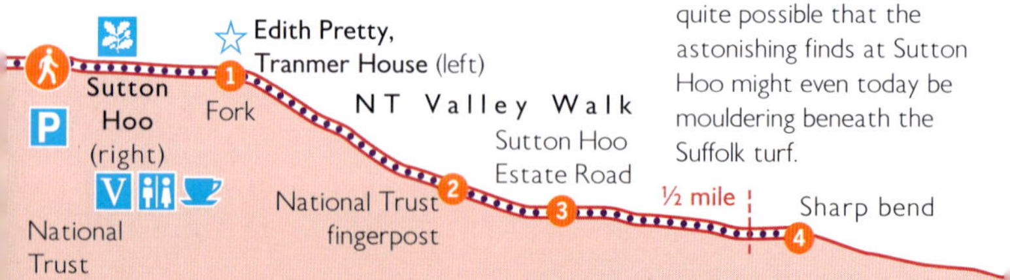

- From the car park, take the exit to the far **left** of the buildings.
- Remain on the broad path as it swings **right** to a fork.

**1** ▶ Take the first path on the **right**, forking **left** after a few paces to head sharply **left** and downhill.
- Continue to a National Trust fingerpost in 200 yards.

50  Short Walks Made Easy

☆ **_Lady Alice Kenlis_**
On the Sutton Hoo side of the Deben lies the hulk of the *Lady Alice Kenlis*. Launched in Glasgow in 1867, she was an iron three-masted steamer. Initially serving as a ferry, she went through numerous owners, eventually fetching up in Bristol as a suction dredger for a sand and gravel company. Ironically, she was scuttled where she lies now around the time Basil Brown was digging for somewhat older ships nearby.

## Anglo-Saxon ship burial

In 1938, Edith Pretty brought in self-taught archaeologist Basil Brown to excavate three of Sutton Hoo's mounds, helped by various estate labourers. They discovered a ship (in Mound 2) and a few finds. The following year, however, they unearthed another Anglo-Saxon ship that promised greater treasures. Professional archaeologists were drafted in and some 263 objects were discovered, many of gold or silver, and there was even a lyre. Among the weapons found was a sensational ceremonial helmet (nationaltrust.org.uk).

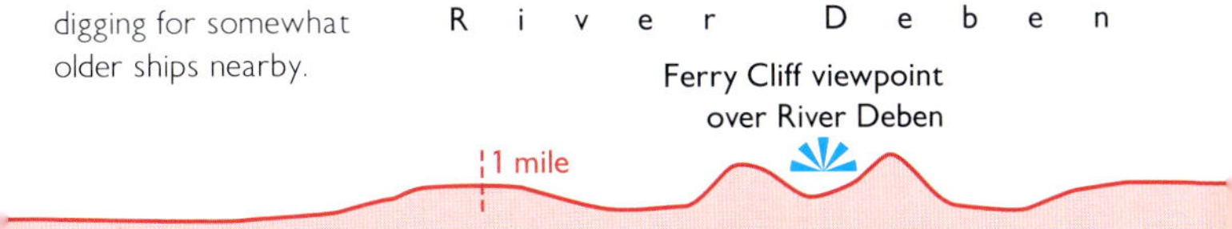

R i v e r    D e b e n

**Ferry Cliff viewpoint over River Deben**

¦1 mile

**2** ▪ At the fingerpost, keep **straight ahead**, following the Valley Walk sign.
▪ Reach an asphalt estate road in about 150 yards.

**3** ▪ Turn **left** along the estate road and continue for 300 yards, still following the Valley Walk sign, to reach a sharp left bend.

**Walk 6** Sutton Hoo

# NATURE NOTES

The Sutton Hoo estate has a patchwork of open, grassy fields and pockets of woodland. Many of the opportunities for spotting wildlife occur on the section of the walk to the River Deben, where mute swans and little egrets are a common sight on and beside the water.

Growing to five feet tall, typically in dense clumps near water, comfrey has large hairy leaves and clusters of tubular flowers that may be purple, pink or creamy-white.

In June and July, on your way to and from the river, examine the heads of ragwort for cinnabar moth caterpillars. Chubby yellow fellows with raised black hoops, they're unmistakeable for anything else. They'll become beautiful cinnabar moths after spending the winter as cocoons. You may also see the comma butterfly, with its white 'comma' on the underside of its hind wings, flitting about above the false oat grass, spear thistle, field bindweed and a species of the unfortunately named genus bastard cabbage, a brassica with small yellow petals.

Field bindweed

2 miles — Mound 2, Anglo-Saxon ship burial (ahead)

Estate road (house, left; sharp bend (right)) ⑤

1½ miles

④ ■ Just before the road bends sharp left by a house, turn **right** down a tarmac drive. Stay on this as it narrows and becomes a grassy path.
■ Follow this path for ⅓ mile to a River Deben viewpoint at Ferry Cliff, walking between fields and skirting a wood before heading up a small rise.
■ After enjoying the Deben views, retrace your steps to the estate road at ④.

52  Short Walks Made Easy

Above: mute swans on the River Deben
Below: cinnabar moth caterpillars

Top: false oat grass
Bottom: comma

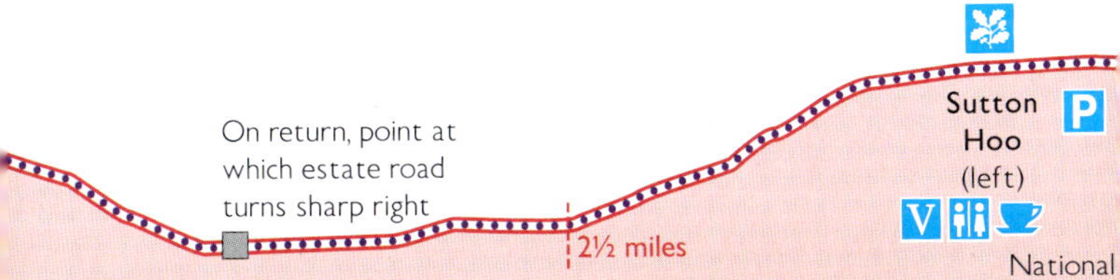

On return, point at which estate road turns sharp right

2½ miles

**Sutton Hoo** (left)

National Trust Sutton Hoo car park

N T  V a l l e y  W a l k

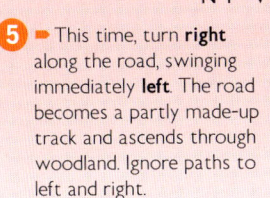

**5** ▶ This time, turn **right** along the road, swinging immediately **left**. The road becomes a partly made-up track and ascends through woodland. Ignore paths to left and right.

▶ When the track emerges from the woods at the top, you'll see the Royal Burial Ground's Mound 2 **ahead**.

▶ Return to **5**; this time stay on the road and retrace your steps back to the start.

Walk 6  Sutton Hoo   53

# WALK 7

# DEDHAM AND FLATFORD

**CATCH A BUS**

### OS information

TM 058333
Explorer 196

**Distance**
4 miles/6.4km

**Time**
2¼ hours

**Start/Finish**
Dedham

**Parking** CO7 6DH
Mill Lane car park

**Public toilets**
Dedham, just south of ❶; opposite the RSPB Flatford Wildlife Garden, near ❻/❼

**Cafés/pubs**
Dedham; National Trust café, Flatford

**Terrain**
Pavement, lane; grassy paths

**Hilliness**
Level throughout

The village of Dedham has proved a magnet for painters. John Constable came here to paint the mill (owned by his father) and the church, ❶. Residents, meanwhile, have included Royal Academy president Sir Alfred Munnings; artists Cedric Morris and Arthur Lett-Haines; and the notorious art forger Tom Keating. This gentle walk through Dedham Vale passes some classic Constable country, taking in Flatford and the River Stour.

⚠ The footpath west of Flatford is liable to flooding after wet weather.

54   Short Walks Made Easy

| Footwear |
|---|
| Spring/Autumn/Winter 🥾 Summer 🩴 |

| 🚌 Public transport |
|---|
| Bus services 80/80A, Colchester to Dedham; 81/81A, Colchester to Manningtree (rail connections at both ends); stop in High Street: hedinghamandchambers.co.uk |

| ♿ Accessibility |
|---|
| Wheelchairs and pushchairs around Dedham, 🚶 to ❷ and ❾ to end, and at Flatford, ❻ to ❼ |

| 🐕 Dogs |
|---|
| A good dog walk. No stiles |

**Did you know?** Turn left just after crossing Flatford Bridge ❻ and you'll find yourself at the RSPB Flatford Wildlife Garden. It's been designed to inspire visitors to make their own gardens or community spaces more wildlife friendly. There's a living willow tunnel, a pond that's home to great crested newts, a cob wall for solitary bees, and much else besides. Events such as butterfly walks and moth identification workshops are held frequently in summer (rspb.org.uk).

**Local legend** The ghost of Eisa, the last woman to have been executed in Essex for witchcraft, is said to haunt The Sun Inn at Dedham. Hanged in the grounds of the pub where she worked, she reportedly appears in a black cloak holding a roll of clothing, sometimes weeping. Ornamental plates have been inexplicably flung about at the inn and the noise of chairs being dragged around has been heard at night.

Scan Me

**Walk 7** Dedham and Flatford

# STORIES BEHIND THE WALK

🌼 **Flatford** This hamlet in Dedham Vale overlooks a somnolent stretch of the River Stour that seems to exist outside the exigencies of time. There has been a mill here since Saxon days and so it's fitting that among the eye-pleasing buildings is Flatford Mill, once owned by the Constable family. If you wish to immerse yourself further in the scene (but hopefully not the river!), rowing boats are available for hire (nationaltrust.org.uk).

☆ **John Constable**
Even today it's easy to see how John Constable (1776–1837) could find in Flatford the inspiration to paint a long series of canvases, some of which have become a staple of English culture. His father, a wealthy corn merchant, owned the now-famous mill. Though it may be hard to believe, Constable was a revolutionary landscape painter in his day — somewhat too revolutionary for art buyers of the time, because he had to make ends meet by painting portraits and country houses.

- At the car park exit, turn **left** along Mill Lane; walk to the T-junction ahead.

**1** ▸ At the junction, with Dedham church ahead, turn **left** onto Royal Square.
▸ Follow the road as it bends sharp **right** and walk to a footpath turning (left) in 100 yards.

**2** ▸ Turn **left** along the public footpath.
▸ Keep **ahead** on this path for just over ⅓ mile as it goes through two gates and a gap in a hedge to another hedge on the far side of the field.

56  Short Walks Made Easy

## ☆ St Edmund Way

Created in honour of England's original patron saint (centuries before St George), this long-distance footpath stretches for 79 miles from Brandon, Norfolk, right through some lovely Suffolk countryside, including the Stour and Lark valleys, as well as Bury St Edmunds, where the saint is buried. You will encounter the St Edmund Way a few miles from its southern end at Manningtree Station in Essex. The trail can be used to link the station with this walk.

## 🏠 Willy Lott's House

This building features in many of John Constable's paintings, including his most famous, *The Hay Wain*. Indeed, if it hadn't been for Constable, it's possible the 16th-century cottage would no longer exist: it was on account of an upsurge of interest in the painter that the cottage was restored in the 1920s. Willy Lott himself was a tenant farmer in Constable's time and is said to have spent just four nights of his entire life away from the cottage.

**RSPB Flatford Wildlife Garden** (left)

**St Edmund Way**

Dedham Old River Bridge and NT Dedham Vale sign

**5** — 1½ miles

**6** — Flatford Bridge — 2 miles

**3** ▸ Go **right** to follow the hedge (left) for 125 yards to a kissing-gate on the left.

**4** ▸ Turn **left** through the kissing-gate and immediately **right**, following a sign to Flatford and Manningtree. Ignore a path, left, after 30 yards.
▸ Continue through two kissing-gates, over a section of concrete track.
▸ Pass through two wide metal gates and bear **right** on a narrow path. Ignore two paths off right, and keep **ahead** across a field to a National Trust Dedham Vale sign and bridge.

**Walk 7** Dedham and Flatford

# NATURE NOTES

The Stour Valley is estimated to be home to 175 species of bird, 1,000 species of moth and over 1,500 species of plant, so you should see flora and fauna of some sort here no matter what time of year you visit. On the river, for example, you may spot banded demoiselles, a large damselfly with a distinctive fluttering flight, and Canada geese. The latter is Britain's largest goose. Introduced from North America about 300 years ago, it only started to become widespread after World War II.

On the river banks, keep your eyes peeled for the delicate pink buds and pastel blue flowers of water forget-me-nots, as well as a fringe of reeds.

Swallows and house martins swoop over the meadows in summer and swifts can be identified by their scythe-like wings and screeching calls.

On the way to Flatford, you'll find meadowsweet, which gained its name from its use as a sweetener of mead, also known as honey wine. You may also see common comfrey, which grows vigorously in any space it can find, and red poppies blooming winningly at field edges.

**Willy Lott's House**

**RSPB Flatford Wildlife Garden** (right)

**Flatford; John Constable**

**Flatford Bridge**

2½ miles

River Stour

St Edmund Way

3 miles

**5** ▶ At the National Trust sign, go through the kissing-gate and cross the bridge into Suffolk over Dedham Old River.

▶ Carry on **forward**, ignoring a path to the right, and reach Flatford Bridge in just over ⅓ mile.

**6** ▶ Go over the bridge and then at the junction turn **right**.

▶ Pass the various attractions until you reach Willy Lott's House. Retrace your steps and re-cross the bridge.

**7** ▶ Turn **right** to go immediately through two gates and into a field, following the direction of the fingerpost (Dedham).

▶ The path runs parallel to the River Stour for ⅔ mile to a gate, a footbridge beyond.

58  Short Walks Made Easy

**Below**: reeds
**Bottom**: poppies

**Top**: swifts
**Bottom**: banded demoiselle

---

footbridge — 3½ miles — River Stour — **9** Dedham Bridge; steps — 4 miles — Mill Lane car park

**8** ► Pass through the gate, **cross** the footbridge and continue **forward** on the St Edmund Way.
► Very shortly afterwards, turn **left**, following a St Edmund Way sign. Stay on this path for ⅔ mile to a road (Dedham Bridge), latterly walking beside the river.

**9** ► At the road bridge, climb six steps, go through a gate and cross the bridge.
► Carry on along Mill Lane to go back into Essex and return to the start.

**Walk 7** Dedham and Flatford  59

Opposite (clockwise):
Carlton Marshes
Visitor Centre café;
Adnams Brewery Shop,
Southwold; The Ship,
Dunwich; Buckenham
Coffee House,
Southwold
This page (clockwise):
The Sun Inn, Dedham;
Two Magpies
Bakery, Southwold;
National Trust café,
Sutton Hoo; Riverside
Tearoom, Orford Quay

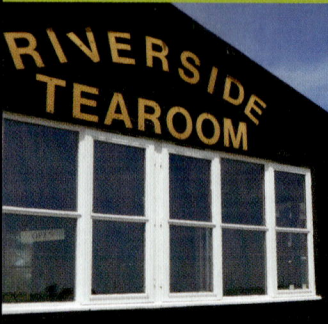

61

# WALK 8

## COLCHESTER TO WIVENHOE

This station-to-station walk visits the top attractions of Roman Britain's first capital: the castle, the priory, the natural history museum and The Minories art gallery. Passing briskly through the city's light industrial quarter, it fetches up on the River Colne for a delightful car-free passage to Wivenhoe, an attractive riverside village. Note that Colchester has two railway stations, Colchester and Colchester Town, which are just over a mile apart. This walk starts from the branch-line terminus Colchester Town.

### OS information
TM 000248
Explorer 184

### Distance
4.2 miles/6.7km

### Time
2½ hours

### Start Colchester Town Station
### Finish Wivenhoe Station

### Parking
CO2 7EF Britannia Car Park, Colchester Town Station; or CO7 9DJ Wivenhoe Station car park

### Public toilets
Colchester Bus Station, near ❷; Castle Park, Colchester, near ❸; Clifton Terrace car park, off High Street, near Wivenhoe Station

### Cafés/pubs
Colchester; Wivenhoe

### Terrain
Paved, asphalt, concrete and cinder pathways

### Hilliness
Very gentle rise ❷ to ❸ and descent ❸ to ❹; level beside River Colne

### Footwear
Year round

**Did you know?** The city's dynamic engineering hub stood just outside Colchester Town. Over the years, production switched from nails and lamp posts, to sewing machines, primitive bicycles, machine tools, World War I artillery shells, engines for D-Day landing craft and, finally, engines for record-breaking Intercity trains. The Britannia works closed in 1981.

**Local legend** Colchester's most often reported spectre haunts Red Lion Yard, just along from the castle (left at ❸). In 1632, a chambermaid called Alice Katherine Miller was pushed out of a window of the Red Lion by her lover, a dastardly act. Aside from Alice's woebegone spirit, the hotel entertains a spectral monk and a phantom boy.

**Public transport**
National rail services to 🚉: thetrainline.com

Bus and national coach services to Colchester Bus Station, near ❷: firstbus.co.uk/essex

**Accessibility**
Suitable for wheelchairs and pushchairs throughout

**Dogs** Welcome but keep on leads – traffic and shared-use cycle path ❺ to ❻ and ❽ to end. No stiles

Walk 8 Colchester to Wivenhoe 63

# STORIES BEHIND THE WALK

☆ **Wivenhoe Trail** From ❹ onwards, start looking out for the installations that make up the Wivenhoe Trail. A mixture of art, history and points of interest, the 15 items en route include a cloth disk to mark Colchester's once-significant textile production; a coal box for the city's railway; a lightship; and a smuggling box. You can pick up a Wivenhoe Trail leaflet from the Tourist Information Centre in Castle Park, passed after ❸.

**St Botolph's Priory** Founded in the late 11th century, the priory provided the Augustinian Order with one of its first toe-holds in England. It was dissolved by Henry VIII in 1536 but some of the church remained in use until it was attacked by Roundhead General Fairfax during the Civil War (english-heritage.org.uk).

*[Map with labels:]*
- Britannia Works ☆
- Colchester Town Station
- St Botolph's Gate plaque (left)
- St Botolph's Priory (right)
- Roman Colchester ☆
- Natural History Museum (left)
- Colchester Castle (ahead)
- The Minories; Firstsite ☆
- ½ mile
- Brook Street; traffic lights ❹
- Sign: Hythe Station, University, Wivenhoe
- Pass under railway bridge ❺
- 1 mile

▶ At the exit from Colchester Town Station, turn **right** and walk the few yards to the corner ahead.

❶ ▶ At the corner, by a large roundabout, turn **right**.
▶ Cross the entrance to Britannia Car Park and bear **right** into St Botolph's St.

64  Short Walks Made Easy

## ☆ Roman Colchester

Camulodunum, as the Romans knew Colchester, was established soon after their conquest of Britain in 43 CE. It began as a legionary fortress but soon became the Roman capital of Britain (at least, those parts of Britain that had been subdued) and home to the immense Temple to the Divine Claudius. However, Boudica, queen of the Iceni, had other ideas. Marching on Camulodunum in her rebellion of 61 CE, she completely destroyed it. London became the capital thereafter.

## 🏰 Colchester Castle

In the 11th century, Colchester became home to the largest Norman keep in Europe. Built on top of the Temple of Claudius, it's extremely well preserved and a visit provides an insight into Norman and Roman life. Exhibits include the Fenwick Hoard of Roman treasure, while daily tours head down into the Roman vaults. Unusually, you can try steering a Roman chariot and firing a ballista too (cimuseums.org.uk).

---

NCR 51 — Bridge – Hythe Station Road ❻ — 1½ miles — Hythe Station (ahead) ❼ ❽ — 2 miles — ❾ Pedestrian crossing, Colne Causeway (A134)

❷ ▶ To visit St Botolph's Priory, after 150 yards, turn **right** onto Priory St.
▶ Back on St Botolph's St, keep **right** and, opposite Short Wyre St, look for the pavement plaque at the site of the Roman St Botolph's Gate.
▶ Carry on as St Botolph's St becomes Queen St and walk to the top.

❸ ▶ The Natural History Museum (looks like a church) is **left**; Colchester Castle is **ahead**.
▶ Resume the walk along High Street, with a Visitor Information Centre (left) and The Minories art gallery and entrance to Firstsite, events and exhibitions centre (right). Continue to the bottom of the hill.

Walk 8 Colchester to Wivenhoe 65

# NATURE NOTES

While there are urban birds such as house sparrows, starlings and feral pigeons in Colchester, the main event for nature spotters is the riverside section to Wivenhoe. You may see a great crested grebe on the Colne, just before it disappears on one of its long dives beneath the surface in search of a meal. If you're lucky, a spotted flycatcher might alight on a tree as you pass through one of the several small copses. And you'll certainly see the reed grass that flanks the river, forming an impenetrable wall between the open water and the shore.

Look out too for red campion, which actually has pink flowers, and hawksbeard, which superficially resembles the dandelion. The most unusual riverside plant you'll see here is dittander. This peppery-tasting salt-tolerant herb flowers in June and July. It's not native to Britain and often escapes gardens to inhabit coastal salt marshes and riversides.

**Dittander**

W i v e n

2½ miles | 3 miles

R i v e r   C o l n e

**4** ▸ At the bottom, cross Brook Street at the traffic lights and pass a red telephone box (right).
▸ Just after the phone box, watch for a sign on the right to Hythe Station, University and Wivenhoe.

**5** ▸ Bear **right** at the sign and follow the same signs (National Cycle Route 51) for ¾ mile, until you pass a closed-off footbridge just before a road bridge near Hythe Station.

**6** ▸ Turn **left** over the road bridge, taking care as you walk along a very narrow pavement to the first turning on the right.

Short Walks Made Easy

**Top left**: great crested grebe
**Bottom left**: reed grass
**Above**: hawksbeard
**Below**: house sparrow

h o e  T r a i l

3½ miles  4 miles

(right)

Wivenhoe Station

**7** ➤ Go **right** into Hawkins Road.
➤ In 350 yards, as the road bends left, look for a footpath on the right.

**8** ➤ Turn **right** on the footpath, between two blocks of flats.
➤ When you reach the River Colne, shortly afterwards, bear **left** along a path. This eventually leads off the river and up onto the Colne Causeway (A134).
➤ Walk **left** to the pedestrian crossing.

**9** ➤ **Cross** the A134 and then keep **ahead** along the Wivenhoe Trail.
➤ Stay on this path for just over 2 miles; it will lead you directly to Wivenhoe Station for a return train to Colchester.

Walk 8  Colchester to Wivenhoe  67

# WALK 9

## WEST MERSEA

Fans of pub quizzes would be wise to squirrel away the following fact: Mersea Island is Britain's most easterly inhabited isle. It's connected to the mainland by a causeway called The Strood that can flood at high tide. The vast majority of its population (roughly 7,000) lives in West Mersea, in the south-west corner. On this walk, you'll experience the whole length of the town's shoreline, starting with its seemingly endless beach huts, before heading across the gentle farmland that surrounds it.

**CATCH A BUS**

### OS information

TM 023124
Explorer 184

**Distance**
4.9 miles/7.9km

**Time**
2¾ hours

**Start/Finish**
West Mersea

**Parking** CO5 8DA
Seaview car park

**Public toilets**
On Victoria Esplanade, near 🚶; Coast Road car park, near ❹

**Cafés/pubs**
West Mersea

**Terrain**
Lanes; grassy and sandy paths; stony track

**Hilliness**
Level throughout

**Footwear**
Winter 🥾
Spring/Summer/Autumn 👟

68   Short Walks Made Easy

## Public transport

Bus services 67, Colchester to East Mersea; 68, Highwoods to West Mersea; 86, Colchester to West Mersea; nearest stop is after ❽, East Road, near The Fox Inn: firstbus.co.uk/essex

## Accessibility

Wheelchairs and pushchairs ❸ to ❺ along Coast Road and The Lane

## Dogs
A good dog walk. No stiles

*Did you know?* In the days prior to household plumbing and hot-and-cold running water, the residents of West Mersea were served by wells. St Peter's Well had the reputation for never running dry and was thus the most important local source of fresh water. It was a hub of the community, a literal watering hole where residents would sit and chat, weave fishing baskets and mend nets.

*Local legend* The route of this walk leaves Monkey Beach at ❶ to head up Monkey Steps. The origin of these simian names has been lost in the mists of time. Apparently, a coastguard lookout was once located here and, according to one story, it looked like a cage containing monkeys (presumably the coastguards themselves). An equally implausible tale claims that an actual cage with monkeys once stood here.

Walk 9 West Mersea

# STORIES BEHIND THE WALK

☆ **West Mersea Lifeboat Station** Founded in 1963, West Mersea became one of the Royal National Lifeboat Institution's very first inshore lifeboat stations. The many valiant rescues carried out by the lifeboat crews include groundings in rough seas, small craft struggling in the midst of storms and, on one occasion, 'a man stranded on Osea Island in a Force 10 Gale'. The station is open to the public at weekends and bank holidays between Easter and mid-October (rnli.org).

☆ **Roman West Mersea** It's not just nearby Colchester (page 65) that can trace its heritage back to the Romans. Near the quayside at West Mersea, archaeologists have discovered Roman buildings, as well as pavements created with small square tiles called *tesserae*, as favoured by the Romans. Further evidence of a possible Roman settlement comes in the form of a nearby burial mound from the era, and traces of an ancient road leading to Colchester.

Seaview car park — Beach huts — ½ mile — West Mersea Beach — 1 mile — Monkey Beach — ❶❷ — ❸ Monkey Steps

→ From the car park, cross Victoria Esplanade and turn **right** along a faded footpath. Alternately grassy and sandy, it runs for ½ mile between two lengthy rows of beach huts.

→ Continue along the beach for another ½ mile to the end of the last wall.

❶ → At the wall end, on Monkey Beach, turn **right** to head towards Monkey Steps.

70  Short Walks Made Easy

### 🏛 Mersea Island Museum

In the heart of West Mersea stands a museum built to represent the history and traditions of the island, whose first settlers arrived as long ago as the Bronze Age. There are exhibits telling the story of local boat-building, fishing, oystering and wild fowling, with frequent talks given by experts. Open May to September, there are quizzes and puzzles on hand to keep children entertained (merseamuseum.org.uk).

☆ **The prolific Reverend Baring-Gould**  One doesn't always think of Victorian clergy as potential Renaissance Men but there's no other term for sometime Mersea Island rector Sabine Baring-Gould. His list of talents included historian, poet, archaeologist, hymn writer and author. Astonishingly, he penned so many novels that at one point the British Museum Library stocked more of his titles than of any other author. He somehow also found time to write the distinctly martial hymn 'Onward Christian Soldiers'.

**2** ► Climb the steps up to Coast Road.

► Alternatively, turn **left** at the bottom of the steps along a boardwalk. This passes the site of St Peter's Well but misses the views from the road, joining Coast Road 300 yards west of **3**.

**3** ► Turn **left** along the pavement beside Coast Road, following it for ¾ mile, passing houseboats, a marina and a RNLI station until you reach its end. Look for no-entry signs on the right.

**Walk 9** West Mersea   71

# NATURE NOTES

Mersea Island can feel like a world apart. Its unusual lack of grey squirrels, for instance, enabled the introduction of red squirrels in 2012.

Look out for lapwings – also known as peewits on account of their call – which can sometimes be seen above the fields around West Mersea. On the shore, meanwhile, the slipper limpet resembles a slipper from underneath. However, the rest of the name is bogus since this snail is not related to the limpet.

The walk will take you past plenty of mallows with their cheery pink and purple flowers; sea mayweed, a large summer-flowering daisy; and hawthorns, whose white blossom in spring is a sign that warmer days are on the way. Peacock and red admiral butterflies, while most common in spring and summer, may also be seen on warmer days at other seasons as they overwinter as adults.

| 2½ miles | B1025 | 3 miles | Dawes Lane | 3½ miles |

**4** ▸ Turn **right**, between the no-entry signs, to walk along The Lane for 300 yards, until it bends sharply right.

**5** ▸ At the bend, leave the road by keeping **ahead** on a footpath to the right of a caravan park entrance.
▸ Pass a woodland cemetery and a large field before emerging onto Colchester Road. Continue **ahead** for 30 yards to a public footpath fingerpost (left).

**6** ▸ Go **left** along a narrow footpath.
▸ In 200 yards, it bears **right** across a field, alongside a hedge, through a gap in it, and crosses another field before becoming a poorly maintained cul-de-sac leading to the B1025.

72  Short Walks Made Easy

Left: peacock butterfly  Right: hawthorn flowers

**Right**: lapwing
**Far right**: red admiral butterfly
**Opposite page**: sea maweed

The Fox Inn (left)

4 miles

Beach ahead

4½ miles

Seaview car park

**7** ▶ Carefully **cross** the road and carry on **ahead** through a gap in a hedge.
▶ Follow a re-routed bridleway that swings **right** to lead round three sides of a field before running arrow-straight for ⅓ mile to reach Dawes Lane.

**8** ▶ Turn **right** along the lane.
▶ At a crossroads, continue **ahead** down Cross Lane. The houses peter out as it becomes an old asphalt road and then a path leading down to the beach.

**9** ▶ Turn **right** just before the beach to walk behind gaily painted beach huts back to the start.
▶ Alternatively, walk along the beach until you see the car park to your **right** through a gap in the beach huts.

Walk 9  West Mersea  73

# WALK 10

## MALDON

The small attractive Essex town of Maldon was once an important port and can trace its lineage back to the Anglo-Saxon Chronicle of 913. This route passes through the town to take in the scene of a momentous incident that occurred that same century: the Battle of Maldon. Note: if you would like to lengthen this walk by visiting Northey Island, the causeway is impassable for approximately three hours either side of high tide. Contact northeyisland@nationaltrust.org.uk for details.

*CATCH A BUS*

### OS information

TL 849069
Explorer 183

**Distance**
4 miles/6.4km

**Time**
2¼ hours

**Start/Finish**
Maldon

**Parking** CM9 5QP
White Horse Lane car park

**Public toilets**
In the car park; Promenade Park, near ❶ and near ❸/❼

**Cafés/pubs**
Maldon

**Terrain**
Pavement; asphalt, stony and grassy paths

**Hilliness**
Mostly level, with one gentle descent to ❸ and one climb ❽ to ❾

**Footwear**
Year round

74  Short Walks Made Easy

*Did you know?* The annual Maldon Mud Race draws thousands of spectators and raises large sums for charity. It began in the 1970s as a low-tide race from Promenade Park across the River Chelmer. Competitors drank a pint of beer from a barrel on the far side before dragging themselves back. There's no beer involved nowadays, but the hundreds of contestants often wear fancy dress that inevitably gets caked in thick gooey mud (maldonmudrace.com).

*Local legend* Maldon's 600-year-old Moot Hall – now mostly used for civil ceremonies – is subject to an impressive range of psychic phenomena. Reports have been made of dark figures materialising, furniture moving about, doors slamming, the sound of footsteps and an unpleasant smell with no apparent origin. Meanwhile, nearby Beeleigh Abbey is reportedly home to the headless ghost of a former owner, which appears on the anniversary of his death.

### Public transport
Bus services 31 and 331, Chelmsford to Burnham; 75, Colchester to Maldon: firstbus.co.uk/essex; 90, Witham to Maldon: stephensonsofessex.com

### Accessibility
Wheelchairs and pushchairs from ⓘ to ⑥, and on the return from the Avenue of Remembrance to the end

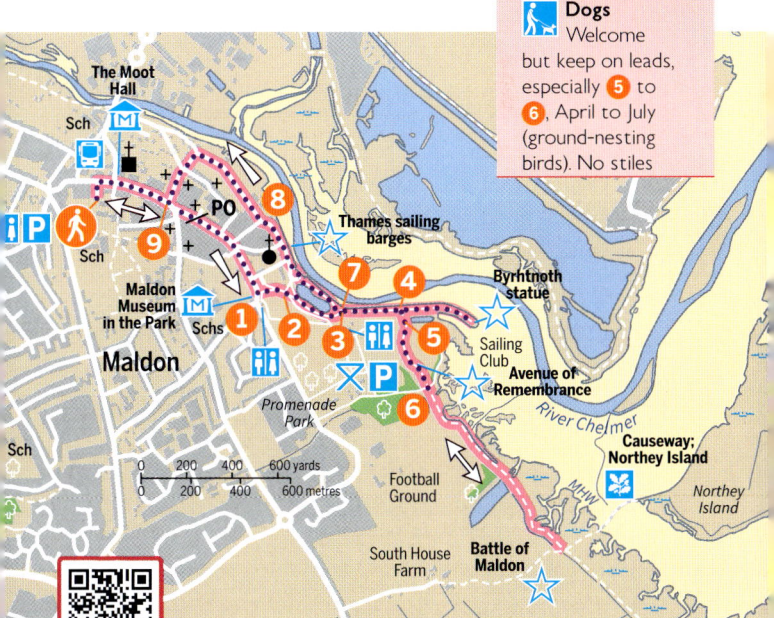

### Dogs
Welcome but keep on leads, especially ⑤ to ⑥, April to July (ground-nesting birds). No stiles

Walk 10 Maldon  75

# STORIES BEHIND THE WALK

☆ **Thames sailing barges** The russet sails of Thames sailing barges were once a common sight on the Thames. Their flat bottoms, shallow draught and nimbleness made them ideal for ferrying goods along the river and its often narrow and shallow tributaries. The Thames Sailing Barge Trust is dedicated to preserving a pair of barges and passing on the know-how to sail them. You can book trips from Maldon, usually over a weekend, sleeping on board (bargetrust.org).

☆ **The Battle of Maldo[n]**
In 991, a Viking force led by Olaf Tryggvason sailed up the River Blackwater and landed on Northey Island. A nearby Saxon elder named Byrhtnot[h] hurriedly pulled together a sm[all] band of men and managed to prevent the Norsemen from crossing the narrow causewa[y] at low tide. Rather than calling for reinforcements, in a stunning display of misguided chivalry, Byrhtnoth agreed to Tryggvason's request for a more formal battle on the mainland. The Saxons were d[...] slaughtered to a man.

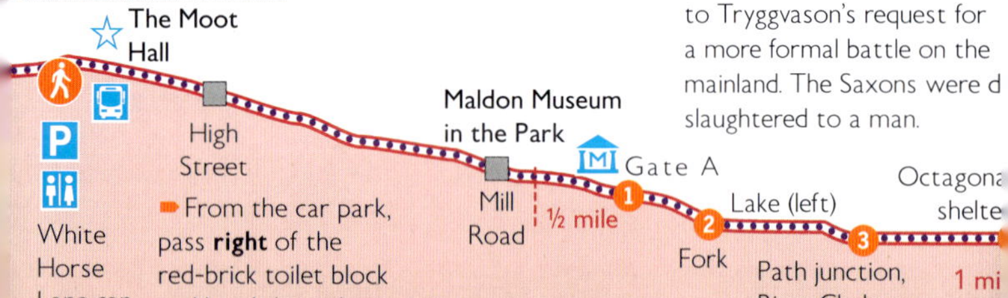

☆ The Moot Hall

White Horse Lane car park

High Street

▪ From the car park, pass **right** of the red-brick toilet block and head through Friars Gate. At the end, turn **right** along High Street.

▪ Carry on for ½ mile, keeping **forward** as the road bends right into Mill Road to reach Promenade Park.

Mill Road

½ mile

Maldon Museum in the Park

Fork

❶ ▪ Turn **left** into Promenade Park via Gate A.
▪ Follow the wide park drive for 150 yards to a fork, where a side path angles downhill.

Gate A

❷ Lake (left)

❸ Octagona[l] shelte[r]

1 mi[le]

Path junction, River Chelmer ahead

Promen[ade]

❷ ▪ Go **left**, downhill, and bear **right** in front of the lake.
▪ Continue on the path as it curves **left** to a junction in front of the River Chelmer.

76  Short Walks Made Easy

## 🏛 Maldon Museum in the Park

Housed in the idiosyncratic Edwardian-era park keeper's lodge in Promenade Park, this century-old museum is devoted to local history. Rather than concentrating on a lot of facts and dates, the exhibits show how Maldon people have lived. The displays include replicas of a vintage shop and a bread oven, the horse-drawn 'Merryweather Manual Machine' used to counter the Great Fire of Maldon (1892), and a Victorian scullery (e-voice.org.uk/maldonmuseuminthepark).

## Northey Island

An estuarine tidal island that shrinks from 300 acres to just 80 at high spring tides, Northey has a long and fascinating history. Landed on by Norsemen, and artificially enlarged by a Dutch civil engineer in the early 1700s, Northey became home to Nobel Peace Prize winner Norman Angell and was bombed by the Luftwaffe (almost certainly by a plane jettisoning its payload while returning home). It's now a remote and rather wonderful wildlife haven owned by the National Trust.

---

Byrhtnoth statue ☆ — Avenue of Remembrance ☆ — **5** Boating lake (left) — 1½ miles — **6** Northey Island fingerpost — 2 miles

Jetty — Boating (right)

e   P a r k

**3** ▶ At the path junction, bear **right**.
▶ Walk with the river (left) for 250 yards to an open-sided octagonal shelter, just before a boating lake.

**4** ▶ To see the statue of Byrhtnoth, continue **forward** until you reach it at the end of the jetty. Return and then turn **left** at the octagonal shelter.
▶ Keep **ahead** and then bear slightly **left** to the Avenue of Remembrance.

Walk 10 Maldon  77

# NATURE NOTES

Arrive at the causeway to Northey Island in summer and you'll find the foreshore carpeted with beautiful lilac-coloured flowers produced in sprays. These are *Limonium vulgareor*, common sea lavender, and they bring a hint of the Mediterranean to this corner of Essex.

Out on the mudflats that are exposed at low tide, both at Northey and in Maldon, you might see oystercatchers streaking through the skies or hear their high-pitched call. In winter, Brent geese come to visit. On the small side for a goose, it has a stubby little bill and a short tail that is white underneath and black on top. The dunlin is a common small wader, starling-sized, and very gregarious, and often forming large flocks.

Shelduck can sometimes be spotted bobbing about on the Chelmer, while Promenade Park is the place to see flocks of starlings, almost oblivious to the humans around them.

**Starlings**

Avenue of Remembrance

Causeway; Northey Island
Battle of Maldon | Battle of Maldon
2½ miles
Promenade Park
Octagonal shelter
3 miles

**5** ▶ Walk along the Avenue of Rembrance to a Northey Island fingerpost at its end.

**6** ▶ Go **forward** to join the footpath to Northey Island. It is ⅔ mile to the causeway.
▶ After enjoying the causeway views, retrace your steps, walking back to the octagonal shelter and going **left** along the promenade to the path junction **3**.

**7** ▶ This time, carry **straight on** along the promenade, keeping **right** of a large black shed.
▶ The path becomes a road – The Hythe – at the Thames Sailing Barge Trust berths.
▶ Walk up to a road corner junction with North Street.

78  Short Walks Made Easy

**Top left**: shelduck
**Top right**: sea lavender
**Left**: Brent geese

**8** ▬ At the junction, continue **forward** along Downs Road (NCN1 sign).
▬ Pass a park and stay on Downs Road as it bends sharp **left** for a brief climb.
▬ At the top, keep **straight ahead** on Butt Lane to reach the High Street.

**9** ▬ Turn **right** on the High Street, by the Rose and Crown, and then retrace your earlier steps to the White Horse Lane car park.

Walk 10 Maldon

## Publishing information

© Crown copyright 2025.
All rights reserved.

Ordnance Survey, OS, and the OS logos are registered trademarks, and OS Short Walks Made Easy is a trademark of Ordnance Survey Ltd.

© Crown copyright and database rights (2025) Ordnance Survey.

ISBN 978 0 319092 92 7
1st edition published by Ordnance Survey 2025.

ordnancesurvey.co.uk

While every care has been taken to ensure the accuracy of the route directions, the publishers cannot accept responsibility for errors or omissions, or for changes in details given. The countryside is not static: hedges and fences can be removed, stiles can be replaced by gates, field boundaries can alter, footpaths can be rerouted and changes in ownership can result in the closure or diversion of some concessionary paths. Also, paths that are easy and pleasant for walking in fine conditions may become slippery, muddy and difficult in wet weather.

If you find an inaccuracy in either the text or maps, please contact Ordnance Survey at os.uk/contact.

All rights reserved. No part of this publication may be reproduced, transmitted in any form or by any means, or stored in a retrieval system without either the prior written permission of the publisher, or in the case of reprographic reproduction a licence issued in accordance with the terms and licences issued by the CLA Ltd.

A catalogue record for this book is available from the British Library.

## Milestone Publishing credits

**Author**: Dixe Wills

**Series editor**: Kevin Freeborn

**Maps**: Cosmographics

**Design and Production**: Patrick Dawson, Milestone Publishing

Printed in India by Replika Press Pvt. Ltd

MIX
Paper | Supporting responsible forestry
FSC™ C016779

## Photography credits

**Front cover**: Joana Kruse/Alamy Stock Photo
**Back cover** cornfield/Shutterstock.com.

All photographs supplied by the author Dixe Wills except page 6 Natasha Sones (Ordnance Survey); page 18 Sue Viccars; 73 ©Vivienne Crow; 79 Fiona Baltrop.

The following images were supplied by:

**Alamy Stock Photo**: page 7 Tim Scrivener; 26 Kumar Sriskandan; 27 Kiko Alvarez; 27 Maria Papworth; 27 Loop Images Ltd; 36 GRANGER - Historical Picture Archive.

**Shutterstock.com**: Page 19 AlekseyKarpenko; 19 Martin Fowler; 19 Menno Schaefer; 41 Dennis Jacobsen; 47 Simonas Minkevicius; 59 Sarah L Woods; 59 Sokolov Alexey; 67 Anton Mizik; 67 Nigel Housden; 73 rorue; 73 Rudmer Zwerver.

**CC0 1.0 Universal Public Domain Dedication**, via Wikimedia Commons: 5, 74 Diane Roberts; 17 Lowestoft Porcelain Factory.

**CC BY-SA 2.0**, via Wikimedia Commons: page 1 Alastair Rae; 17 Adrian S Pue; 70 Simon Frost.

**Public domain, via Wikimedia Commons**: 16 Henry Wyndham Phillips.